RECORD GROUP 125
Records of the Judge Advocate General (Navy)

PC 32

Preliminary Checklist of the Records of the
Office of the Judge Advocate General (Navy), 1799–1943

Compiled by James R. Masterson
Records Control Unit
December 1945

and

NM 55

Supplement to the Preliminary Checklist of the Records of the
Office of the Judge Advocate General (Navy)

Compiled by Harry Schwartz
Records Control Unit
1965

HERITAGE BOOKS
2012

HERITAGE BOOKS
AN IMPRINT OF HERITAGE BOOKS, INC.

Books, CDs, and more—Worldwide

For our listing of thousands of titles see our website
at
www.HeritageBooks.com

A Facsimile Reprint
Published 2012 by
HERITAGE BOOKS, INC.
Publishing Division
100 Railroad Ave. #104
Westminster, Maryland 21157

Originally published
National Archives Library
1945 and 1965

International Standard Book Numbers
Paperbound: 978-0-7884-3479-2
Clothbound: 978-0-7884-9478-9

CONTENTS

Page

INTRODUCTION v

CHECKLIST OF THE RECORDS 1

I. Records Transferred to the Office of the Judge
    Advocate General 1

    A. Records Created by the Office of the Secretary of
       the Navy, 1799-1874 1
       1. Records Relating to Personnel 1
       2. Records Relating to Contracts 2
       3. Records Relating to Prize Vessels and Prize
         Cargoes 2
       4. Other Records 3
    B. Records Created Elsewhere Than in the Office of
       the Secretary of the Navy 4

II. Records Created by the Office of the Judge Advocate
    General, 1865-1866, 1877-1940 4

    A. General Records, 1865-1866, 1879-1911 5
    B. Personnel Records, 1841-1943 9
       1. Records Relating to General Courts Martial,
         Courts of Inquiry, Boards of Investigation,
         and Boards of Inquest, 1841-1943 10
       2. Records Relating to Summary Courts Martial and
         Deck Courts, 1855-1930 14
       3. Records Relating to Examining Boards and Retir-
         ing Boards, 1836-1941 16
       4. Other Personnel Records, 1860-1931 18
    C. Financial Records, 1869-1943 22
    D. Records Relating to Patents, 1907-1942 26
    E. Records Relating to Opinions and Decisions, 1856-
       1911 30
    F. Other Records, 1863-1929 31

III. Records of Boards and Other Special Units Concerned
    With Matters Under the Cognizance of the Judge
    Advocate General, 1896-1933 32

    Board of Examining Professors in Mathematics 32
    Board To Examine Into Certain Accusations Against
       Officers and Employees of the Department of Steam
       Engineering, New York Navy Yard 33
    Board on Revision of the Navy Regulations 33
    Court of Inquiry in the Case of R. A. Winfield S.
       Schley 33
    Examining Board of Ordnance Draftsmen 33

Naval Disciplinary Barracks, Port Royal, S. C. 34
Naval Disciplinary Barracks, Puget Sound, Wash. 34
Board on Valuation of Commandeered Property 34
Legal Section, Force Commander's Office, United States
    Naval Forces Operating in European Waters 35
Paris Naval Board on Claims 36
London Naval Board on Claims 37
Board on Submarine Claims 39
Interdepartmental Radio Board 39
Board To Consider Claims of the Electric Boat Company
    Under Contracts for Submarines 39
East Camp Claims Board 40
Cancellation Board 40
Naval War Claims Board 41
Naval Membership of the American Delegation to the
    International Conference on Safety of Life at Sea . . 42
Board of Appraisal for the Appalachian Electric Power
    Company 43
Commission for Hearing and Determining of Claims by
    British Nationals 43

APPENDIXES 44
    A. Records of the Office of the Judge Advocate General
        in the General File of the Office of the Secretary
        of the Navy 44
    B. Cases in "Navy Yard Cases" (Entry 29) 47
    C. Subject Headings in the Subject File of the Legal Sec-
        tion, Force Commander's Office, United States Naval
        Forces Operating in European Waters, 1918-1921 (Entry
        136) 49

INTRODUCTION

During the first sixty-seven years after the establishment of the Department of the Navy the legal matters under the cognizance of the Secretary of the Navy were not separated for administrative purposes from other business handled directly by the Office of the Secretary of the Navy. An act of March 2, 1865, authorized the President to appoint an officer in the Navy Department to be called the Solicitor and Naval Judge-Advocate General. This official was transferred, with the title of the Naval Solicitor, to the Department of Justice by the act creating that Department, June 22, 1870; but all functions pertaining to the trial, examination, promotion, and retirement of Naval and Marine Corps personnel were retained by the Navy Department. The Office of the Naval Solicitor was abolished by an act of June 19, 1878. In the meantime a Naval Solicitor and Judge Advocate General of the Navy Department had been designated by a circular issued by the Secretary of the Navy on March 14, 1877. The title of this official was changed to Acting Judge Advocate by a circular of July 2, 1878. An act of June 8, 1880, authorized the President to appoint in the Navy Department a Judge Advocate General of the Navy with the rank of a captain in the Navy or a colonel in the Marine Corps. Since that date the continuity of the office has remained unbroken.

During the years from 1908 to 1921 the functions of the Office of the Judge Advocate General included only matters relative to Naval and Marine Corps personnel. The civil functions formerly exercised by the Office were transferred to the Office of the Solicitor of the Navy. The establishment of the latter Office was authorized by an act of May 22, 1908, and the operations of the Office began on July 1 of the same year. The two Offices were independent of each other, each being responsible only to the Secretary of the Navy. On September 1, 1921, this separation was ended, and by order of the Secretary of the Navy the Office of the Solicitor was merged into the Office of the Judge Advocate General.

Except for the years from 1908 to 1921 the functions of the Office of the Judge Advocate General have been changed only in minor respects. They have related in general to the trial and punishment of Navy and Marine Corps personnel for violations of law and regulations, the promotion and retirement of officers of the Navy and the Marine Corps, claims and suits to which the Navy Department was a party, contracts requiring the Department's action, muniments pertaining to naval real estate, and all other matters of law, legislation, regulations, and discipline.

In United States Navy Regulations, 1920, revised in 1932, Article 469, the duties of the Judge Advocate General were defined as follows:

(1) The Judge Advocate General of the Navy shall, in accordance with the statute creating his office, have cognizance of all matters of law arising in the Navy Department and shall perform such other duties as may be assigned him by the Secretary of the Navy.

(2) The duties of the Judge Advocate General of the Navy shall be to revise and report upon the legal features of and to have recorded the proceedings of all courts-martial, courts of inquiry, boards of investigation and inquest, and boards for the examination of officers for retirement and promotion in the naval service; to prepare charges and specifications for courts-martial, and the necessary orders convening courts-martial, in cases where such courts are ordered by the Secretary of the Navy; to prepare courts-martial orders promulgating the final action of the reviewing authority in general courts-martial cases, except those of enlisted men convened by officers other than the Secretary of the Navy; to prepare the necessary orders convening courts of inquiry and boards for the examination of officers for promotion and retirement, for the examination of all candidates for appointment as officers in the naval service, other than midshipmen, and in the Naval Reserve Force, where such courts and boards are ordered by the Secretary of the Navy, and to conduct all official correspondence relating to such courts and boards.

(3) It shall also be the duty of the Judge Advocate General of the Navy to examine and report upon all questions relating to rank and precedence, to promotions and retirements, and to the validity of the proceedings in courts-martial cases; all matter relating to the supervision and control of naval prisons and prisoners, including prisoners of war; the removal of the mark of desertion; the correction of records of service of the naval personnel; certification of discharge in true name; pardons; the interpretation of statutes; references to the general accounting officers of the Treasury; proceedings in the civil courts by or against the Government or its officers; preparation of advertisements, proposals, and contracts; insurance; patents; the sufficiency of official contracts, and other bonds and guarantees; claims by or against the Government; and to conduct the correspondence respecting the foregoing duties, including the preparation for submission to the Attorney General of all questions which the Secretary of the Navy may direct to be so submitted.

(4) It shall be the duty of the Judge Advocate General of the Navy to examine and report upon all bills and resolutions introduced in Congress and referred to the Department for report; to draft all proposed legislation arising in the Navy Department; and to conduct the correspondence in connection with these duties.

(5) The study of international law is assigned to the office of the Judge Advocate General of the Navy. He shall examine and report upon questions of international law as may be required.

(6) He shall be charged, under the special instructions of the Secretary of the Navy, with the searching of titles, purchase, sale, transfer, and other questions affecting lands and buildings pertaining to the Navy, and with the care and preservation of all muniments of title to land acquired for naval uses.

The duties of the Solicitor of the Navy were defined as follows in Regulations for the Government of the Navy of the United States, 1909, Article 13:

>   (1) It shall be the duty of the Solicitor to examine and report upon questions of law, including the drafting and interpretations of statutes, and matters submitted to the accounting officers, not relating to the personnel; preparation of advertisements, proposals, and contracts; insurance; patents; the sufficiency of official, contract, and other bonds and guarantees; acquisition of and questions affecting lands; proceedings in the civil courts by or against the Government or its officers; claims by or against the Government; questions submitted to the Attorney-General; bills and Congressional resolutions and inquiries not relating to the personnel and not elsewhere assigned; and to conduct the correspondence respecting the foregoing duties. Opinions relating to the personnel shall, when received, be referred by the Solicitor to the Bureau of Navigation via the office of the Judge Advocate General.
>
>   (2) He shall be charged under the special instructions of the Secretary of the Navy with the purchase, sale, transfer, and other questions affecting lands and buildings pertaining to the Navy, and with the care and preservation of all muniments of title to land acquired for naval uses.
>
>   (3) He shall also render opinions upon any matter or question of law when directed to do so by the Secretary of the Navy.

As all functions separated from the Office of the Judge Advocate General in 1908 were returned to it in 1921, the records of the Office of the Solicitor are treated in this checklist as records of the Office of the Judge Advocate General, and no effort is made to distinguish between the records of the two Offices. Many series of records begun in one Office were continued or completed in the other; and the records of both are intermingled to such a degree that even if their separation seemed desirable it would not be feasible.

Administratively the Office of the Judge Advocate General has always been within the Office of the Secretary of the Navy. Its records, therefore, are parts of the records of the Secretary's Office; but in this checklist it has occasionally been considered convenient to ignore this distinction and to refer to the Office of the Secretary and to the Office of the Judge Advocate General as if they were wholly separate and coordinate administrative units. The Office of the Judge Advocate General has possessed such a degree of autonomy and its records are of such distinct character and of such quantity that it has appeared desirable to the National Archives to consider the records of the Office as constituting a separate record group.

The records described in this checklist form three groups: records transferred from other units of the Navy Department to the Office of the Judge Advocate General, records created by that Office, and records of boards and other special units concerned with matters under the cognizance of the Judge Advocate General. They constitute those parts of Record Group

125, Records of the Office of the Judge Advocate General (Navy), that were transferred to the National Archives before July 1, 1945. They have a total linear measurement of 3,953 feet and a total bulk of 2,696 cubic feet.

Many of the records that were once in the custody of the Office of the Judge Advocate General, having been inherited or created by it, are now in Record Group 45, Naval Records Collection of the Office of Naval Records and Library. They are entered in this checklist for purposes of cross reference. Such entries are enclosed in brackets and contain only the title of each series of records, its inclusive dates, the number of volumes or other units of which it consists, and the entry number (e.g., NRC 249) assigned to it in a preliminary checklist of the Naval Records Collection, which has been multilithed by the National Archives.

Each entry for records in Record Group 125 describes a unit of records conceived (for purposes of the present checklist) as forming a series, designated by a serial number at the end of the first paragraph of the entry. Subseries are designated by numerals in parentheses. When the backstrip title of a bound series is not identical or nearly identical with the title assigned to the series in this checklist, the backstrip title is cited within quotation marks if it appears useful as a brief designation or as a means of physically identifying volumes. The word "indexed," when entered in the first paragraph, indicates that the volume or volumes forming the series contain an index in each volume. The quantity of each series is expressed by its linear measurement, regarded as the height of the pile that would be formed if the records constituting the series were laid one upon another.

As many of the "records of" one agency consist of materials that were filed as records by another agency, the words "created by" are used in this checklist to indicate the agency by which the record character of these materials was established; they should not be understood as referring to an agency by which they were produced but not retained and filed for record purposes.

PRELIMINARY CHECKLIST

I. RECORDS TRANSFERRED TO THE OFFICE OF THE JUDGE ADVOCATE GENERAL

The records listed in this section did not originate as records in the Office of the Judge Advocate General but were transferred to it. They are therefore records of the Office only in the sense that they relate to its functions, came into its possession, and were maintained by it with the records that it created. Of the series listed, all but five were later transferred to the Naval Records Collection of the Office of Naval Records and Library (Record Group 45), of which they are now a part.

A. Records Created by the Office of the Secretary of the Navy, 1799-1874

The records listed below were transferred to the Office of the Judge Advocate General from the Office of the Secretary of the Navy, in which they had been filed before the several kinds of legal functions of the Office of the Secretary to which these records pertain were formally assigned, in 1880, to the newly established Office of the Judge Advocate General. Other records of similar origin that were continued by the Office of the Judge Advocate General as unbroken series are listed in Part II of this checklist.

1. Records Relating to Personnel

ROUGH INDEX TO RECORDS OF GENERAL COURTS MARTIAL AND COURTS OF INQUIRY. June 1799 - Mar. 1861. 1 vol. 3/4 in. Arranged by first letter of names of men tried or investigated, thereunder chronologically.   1
    Gives only the name of the man tried or investigated, his rank or rating, and the number of his case. The volume includes cases 1-3072 described in NRC 294.

[Index to Records of General Courts Martial and Courts of Inquiry. June 1799 - Dec. 1860. 1 vol. NRC 295.]

[Register of Judgments and Sentences of Courts Martial and Courts of Inquiry. Aug. 1800 - Jan. 1822. 1 vol. NRC 296.]

[Records of Proceedings of Courts of Inquiry Convened under the Act of January 16, 1857. Feb. 1857 - Feb. 1859. 24 vols. NRC 145.]

[Records of Proceedings of a General Court Martial in the Case of Commo. Charles Wilkes. Mar. 9 - Apr. 26, 1864. 3 vols. NRC 162.]

[Record of Proceedings of a General Court Martial in the Case of Franklin W. Smith and Benjamin G. Smith. Sept. 15, 1864 - Jan. 30, 1865. 10 vols. NRC 163.]

RECORDS OF THE BOARD OF EXAMINERS FOR ASSISTANT NAVAL CONSTRUCTORS.
     Feb. 6 - Mar. 3, 1866. Envelopes and loose papers. 1 ft. 10
    in. Unarranged.   2
   Journal of proceedings of the Board; correspondence, including applications, petitions, and replies thereto; and examination papers.

[Report from the Board for the Examination of Volunteer Officers for
    Admission to the Regular Navy. Dec. 5, 1867. 6 vols. NRC 166.]

ORDERS RECEIVED FROM THE SECRETARY OF THE NAVY BY THE BOARD FOR THE
    EXAMINATION OF OFFICERS FOR PROMOTION UNDER THE ACT OF APRIL 21,
    1864. Sept. 30 - Dec. 21, 1868. 1 adhesive binder. 1 in. Ar-
    ranged chronologically.   3
   By its precept, Sept. 30, 1868, the Board was directed to convene at
the Philadelphia Navy Yard to investigate and report on such cases as
might be referred to it. The President of the Board was Capt. William
H. Macomb, succeeded by Commo. Thomas O. Selfridge and Commo. George F.
Emmons.

[Letters Sent by the Board for the Examination of Officers for Promotion
    under the Act of April 21, 1864. Oct. 1868 - Apr. 1869. 1 vol.
    NRC 368.]

[Letters from the Naval Examining Board at Washington. Jan. 1870 - Dec.
    1872. 3 vols. NRC 167.]

[Report from the Board Appointed under the Resolution of July 1, 1870,
    on Officers not Promoted under the Act of July 25, 1866. Dec. 21,
    1871. 2 vols. NRC 168.]

2. Records Relating to Contracts

[Ledger of Contracts Entered into by the Navy Department. Nov. 1834 -
    Mar. 1852. 2 vols. NRC 141.]

[Contracts for Transportation of Mail and for Manufacture of Parts of
    Ships. Apr. 1847 - Oct. 1860. 1 vol. NRC 143.]

[Contracts for Manufacture of Machinery for Vessels. Aug.-Dec. 1862.
    1 vol. NRC 155.]

[Confidential Letters from Special Investigators of Frauds in Naval Pro-
    curement. Feb.-Dec. 1864. 2 vols. NRC 161.]

[Letters Sent by William E. Chandler, Special Counsel for the Navy De-
    partment, and George H. Chandler, Investigating Frauds Connected with
    War Contracts. Dec. 1864 - Apr. 1865. 1 vol. NRC 164.]

3. Records Relating to Prize Vessels and Prize Cargoes

[Rough Lists of Capturing and Captured Vessels. 1861-65. 5 vols. NRC
  146.]

[Summaries of Proceedings for the Adjudication of Prizes in Courts of the District of New York. May 1861 - Jan. 1863. 1 vol. NRC 147.]

[Summaries of District-Court Proceedings in Prize Cases. June 1861 - July 1867. 7 vols. NRC 148.]

[Register of Prize Cases. June 1861 - Dec. 1874. 14 vols. NRC 149.]

[Index to Register of Prize Cases. 1861-68. 1 vol. NRC 150.]

[Register of Prizes. Aug. 1861 - Dec. 1863. 1 vol. NRC 151.]

[Correspondence with Consuls Relating to Blockade Runners and to Vessels Fitted out Abroad to Serve the Confederate States. Sept. 1861 - June 1863. 1 vol. NRC 152.]

[Register of Prizes. Sept. 1861 - Oct. 1864. 1 vol. NRC 153.]

[Lists of Officers and Crews Entitled to Share in Proceeds of Prizes. Jan. 1862 - Mar. 1866. 12 vols. NRC 154.]

[Decrees of Distribution of Prize Moneys. Sept. 1862 - Dec. 1869. 6 vols. NRC 157.]

[Index to Prizes. Nov. 1862 - June 1871. 1 vol. NRC 159.]

4. Other Records

[Letters from the Attorney General. June 1807 - Nov. 1825. 1 vol. NRC 139.]

[Notes and Extracts of Decisions on Cases Referred to and from the Secretary of the Navy, Feb. 1834 - Dec. 1848, and Notes on Navy Rations and Transportation Pay, July 1831 - Aug. 1857. 1 vol. NRC 140.]

[Miscellaneous Case Files. Aug. 1846 - July 1874. 7 vols. NRC 142.]

MISCELLANEOUS RECORDS RELATING TO MATTERS OF NAVAL DISCIPLINE ("Miscellaneous Subjects. Arrests, Courts Martial, Dismissals, Desertions, Suspensions"). Dec. 1860 - Apr. 1874. 1 vol. 1 1/2 in. Arranged more or less chronologically. Indexed.
Of the same character as the preceding series, of which this volume was apparently part before the other volumes were added to the Naval Records Collection.

[Reports of Officers on Corporal Punishment and the Spirit Ration. Jan.-Feb. 1850. 1 vol. NRC 144.]

[Register of Prisoners Captured on Blockade-Runners. Sept. 1862 - July 1865. 1 vol. NRC 156.]

[Letters Received Relating to Union Prisoners of War. Nov. 1862 - July 1865. 1 vol. NRC 158.]

[Letters Received Relating to Confederate Prisoners of War. Mar. 1863 - July 1865. 4 vols. NRC 160.]

[Index to Letters Received by the Secretary of the Navy Relative to Claims. Jan. 1865 - May 1876. 6 vols. NRC 165.]

B. Records Created Elsewhere Than in the Office of the Secretary of the Navy

The records listed below were created by the Board of Navy Commissioners, the Bureau of Yards and Docks, and the Department of State. The dates and circumstances of their transfer to the Office of the Judge Advocate General are not known.

REGISTER OF DOCUMENTS RELATING TO PUBLIC REAL ESTATE IN CHARGE OF THE BUREAU OF YARDS AND DOCKS. Apr. 1766 - Mar. 1902. 2 vols. 4 in.
Arranged by shore establishments, thereunder by document number. 5
One volume, without backstrip title, appears to be the original, Apr. 1766 - Mar. 1902; the other is labeled "Index Book of Deeds & Documents respecting Public Real Estate in Charge of the Bureau of Y'ds & Docks, U. S. Navy Depart., Duplicate, Bureau of Yards & Docks," Apr. 1766 - Aug. 1882. The second is apparently an incomplete copy of the first. The volumes are with records of the Judge Advocate General's Office and are therefore presumed to have been transferred to that Office because of its cognizance over the legal aspects of Naval real estate. Possibly the original (of which the compilation was begun at an unknown date) was transferred in 1882 and continued by the Office of the Judge Advocate General. The register gives the number of each document, its date, and an abstract of its contents. The papers referred to were evidently filed in numbered bundles, classified by shore establishments and with separate numbers for the documents in each bundle. These papers are not known to be in the National Archives.

[Letters Received by the Secretary of State from Collectors of Customs Relating to Commissions of Privateers. 1812-15. 6 vols. NRC 388.]

[Index to Letters Received by the Secretary of State from Collectors of Customs Relating to Commissions of Privateers. 1812-15. 1 vol. NRC 389.]

[Contracts. June 1794 - Dec. 1842. 15 vols. NRC 235.]

[Contractors' Bonds. Apr. 1820 - Mar. 1842. 5 vols. NRC 245.]

[Data Relative to Contracts. July 1820 - Nov. 1821, Nov. 1836 - May 1839. 1 vol. NRC 246.]

II. RECORDS CREATED BY THE OFFICE OF THE JUDGE ADVOCATE GENERAL, 1865-1866, 1877-1940

The records listed in this section either originated as records in the Office of the Judge Advocate General or were continued in that Office as unbroken series after being transferred thither from the Office of the Secretary of the Navy. The introduction to this checklist sets forth briefly the administrative history of the Office of the Judge Advocate General (established by an act of June 8, 1880); the Offices of his predecessors, the Solicitor and Naval Judge-Advocate General (in the Navy Department Mar. 1865 - June 1870), the Naval Solicitor and Judge Advocate General of the Navy Department (Mar. 1877 - July 1878), and the Acting Judge Advocate (July 1878 - June 1880); and the Office of the Solicitor of the Navy Department (July 1908 - Aug. 1921). For convenience all these Offices are hereafter designated collectively as the Office of the Judge Advocate General.

As the Office of the Judge Advocate General has been a comparatively small and homogeneous organization, no effort is made to attribute its records to the several administrative units within the Office. Instead, the records are listed according to the main subjects to which they pertain: general matters, discipline, finance (contracts, claims, and real estate), patents, opinions and decisions, and other subjects. Many of the records are not externally recognizable as records of the Office of the Judge Advocate General but appear on first inspection to be records of the Office of the Secretary of the Navy. Since 1877, however, the Secretary of the Navy has delegated to the Judge Advocate General all administrative details relating to the subjects mentioned above. Final action in such matters has usually been reserved for the Secretary himself, or has been taken by the Judge Advocate General only in the name of the Secretary and by his specific instructions; but the preliminary papers for the Secretary's perusal have been prepared by the Judge Advocate General, many of the Secretary's decisions and endorsements have been drafted by the Judge Advocate General, and the latter has been responsible for maintaining the records that relate to the subjects under his cognizance.

A. General Records, 1865-1866, 1879-1911

The records listed in this subsection relate to the general activities of the Office of the Judge Advocate General. Only one volume consisting solely of records of the Office of the Solicitor and Naval Judge-Advocate General (Entry 6) is known to exist. For a time after the appointment of the Naval Solicitor and Judge Advocate General (Mar. 14, 1877) most of the correspondence of that official was bound with correspondence of the Secretary of the Navy in series that now form part of the Naval Records Collection of the Office of Naval Records and Library. The first recognizable separate files began in December 1879. The last general file of the Office of the Judge Advocate General that is described in this checklist was discontinued on March 31, 1908, and for thirty-four years thereafter the general correspondence of the Office was filed with that of the Office of the Secretary of the Navy (Record Group 80). Details regarding the consolidated file are set forth in Appendix A. Records of the Office of the Judge Advocate General other than general records continued to be filed separately from those of the Office of the Secretary.

LETTERS SENT BY THE SOLICITOR AND NAVAL JUDGE-ADVOCATE GENERAL ("Solicitor's Letters, No. 1"). Mar. 1865 - Jan. 1866. 1 vol. 2 1/2
in. Handwritten copies. Arranged chronologically. Indexed.   <u>6</u>
   Reports to the Secretary of the Navy and copies of endorsements and of
letters to district attorneys, from William E. Chandler, Mar. 21 - June
17, 1865, and John A Bolles, July 22, 1865 - Jan. 3, 1866.

REGISTER OF LETTERS RECEIVED. Jan. 1876 - Sept. 1880. 1 vol. 2 1/2
in. Arranged chronologically. Indexed.   <u>7</u>
   Gives date of receipt of letter, name or title of writer, abstract,
and action taken. The nature of the register is not entirely clear. It
was begun as a register of letters received by the Secretary of the Navy
relating to courts martial, prisoners, claims, prize money, and other
subjects that were later under the cognizance of the Judge Advocate General. The later letters were apparently received by the Judge Advocate
General and referred by him to other officials. The title "Papers and
Letters Received" is on the front cover. All that is left of the backstrip
title is "R— Co— Ma—," probably a remnant of "Record of Courts Martial,"
though this title would not accurately designate the contents of the volume.

LETTERS SENT ("Letter Book, N°. 1"). Dec. 1879 - Jan. 1883. 1 vol.
2 1/2 in. Handwritten copies. Arranged chronologically.
Indexed.   <u>8</u>
   From Col. William B. Remey, USMC, Acting Judge Advocate, later Judge
Advocate General, to officers, Congressmen, and others. Since the copies
occupy only 73 pages, it seems probable that only selected letters are
included, but no criterion of choice is found. The letters are not confidential.

LETTERS SENT ("Letters"). Dec. 1879 - Dec. 1911. 48 vols. 5 ft.
5 in. Press copies. Arranged chronologically. Indexed.   <u>9</u>
   Letters (including endorsements and telegrams) relative to discipline,
contracts, service records, and other matters. Their subjects were
gradually narrowed as other series of press copies of letters sent were
begun.

LETTERS RECEIVED. Dec. 1879 - June 1883, with a few letters as early
as May 1877. Envelopes and folded papers. 13 ft. 9 in. Arranged by first letter of correspondents' names or titles; thereunder unarranged. Registered in part in Entry 7; indexed in part
in Entries 11 and 12.   <u>10</u>
   The letters relate to all matters under the cognizance of the Judge
Advocate General. Apparently the file was begun in Dec. 1879, and then
or later a few letters of earlier date were inserted. Very few of the
letters are subsequent to 1881. The letters under A and B in the alphabet have disappeared.

INDEX TO LETTERS RECEIVED ("Key to Letters Received"). July 1880 -
June 1883. 1 vol. 2 in. Arranged by first letter of correspondents' names or titles, thereunder chronologically.   <u>11</u>
   Gives date of receipt, file number, name and address of writer, date
and purport of letter, and action taken (whether filed or referred).

INDEX TO LETTERS REFERRED ("Key to Papers Referred"). Sept. 1880 – June
1883. 1 vol. 3 in. Arranged by first letter of correspondents'
names or titles, thereunder chronologically.   12
   Gives date of receipt, writer's name, subject, to whom referred, when
returned, and how disposed of.

GENERAL FILE. July 1883 – Dec. 1904. Folded papers. 411 ft. Arranged
by serial number, with separate sets of numbers for 1883-84, 1885-
86, and each calendar year thereafter. Registered in Entry 15;
indexed in Entries 14 and 17.   13
   Letters received folded with press or carbon copies of letters sent.
Many letters bearing numbers belonging to this series were filed in
various other series (Entries 69, 88, 89, 92, 118, 125).

INDEX TO GENERAL FILE. July 1883 – Dec. 1889. 1 vol. 3 in. Arranged
in periods (1883-84, 1885, 1886, 1887, 1888, 1889), thereunder by
first letter of subject or of correspondents' names or titles,
thereunder chronologically.   14
   Gives subject or name, file number, and a very brief indication of
contents of letter. Subject entries are in red, name entries in black.

REGISTER OF LETTERS RECEIVED ("Letters Received"). July 1883 – Dec.
1904. 19 vols. 5 ft. 6 in. Arranged chronologically.   15
   Gives date of receipt, file number, name and address of writer, date
and purport of letter, and action taken (whether filed or referred). The
first volume is labeled "2." Vol. 1 may have been lost, or it may have
been the series described in Entry 11 ("Key to Letters Received"), which
is labeled "1" and may have been regarded as a register in that it cor-
responded to the alphabetical order of the letters received before July
1883.

COMMUNICATIONS TO THE SECRETARY OF THE NAVY ("Letters, Memoranda, Reports,
Opinions, &c." and other titles). July 1885 – Feb. 1912. 16 vols.
2 ft. Press copies. Arranged chronologically. Indexed.   16
   From the Judge Advocate General, relative chiefly to matters of discipline, contracts, and law.

INDEX TO LETTERS RECEIVED. Jan. 1890 – Dec. 1904. 15 vols. 3 ft. 4
in. Arranged chronologically by volumes, thereunder by first
letter of subjects (in red) and of correspondents' names or
titles (in black), thereunder chronologically.   17
   Gives writer's name or title or name of subject, abstract, and file
number. The volumes are numbered 1-15 (one for each calendar year) but
are a continuation of Entry 14.

ENDORSEMENTS. Sept. 1890 – Dec. 1892. 2 vols. 3 1/2 in. Press copies.
Arranged chronologically. First volume indexed.   18
   Relative chiefly to discipline and contracts. Some of the endorse-
ments are signed by the Secretary of the Navy.

UNOFFICIAL LETTERS SENT. Apr. 1892 – Oct. 1909. 5 vols. 7 in. Press
copies. All but last volume indexed.   19
   Sent by (1) various Judge Advocates and E. P. Hanna, Chief Clerk of
the Office of the Judge Advocate General (Solicitor on and after July 1,

1908), Apr. 1892 - May 1909 ("Letters," 1 vol.); (2) Capt. Samuel C. Lemly, Oct. 1892 - June 1904 ("Letters," 2 vols.); (3) Capt. S. W. B. Diehl, June 1904 - Nov. 1907 (no title, 1 vol.); and (4) Capt. Edward H. Campbell, Nov. 1907 - Oct. 1909 (no title, 1 vol.). Informal communications to officers, business letters, letters to friends and relatives, letters of congratulation, and the like.

CONFIDENTIAL LETTERS SENT. Sept. 1894 - Mar. 1904. 1 vol. 1 1/2 in. Press copies. Arranged chronologically. Indexed.   20
  Addressed chiefly to officers, enlisted men, and Congressmen, and concerned chiefly with matters of discipline.

OFFICE FILE OF CAPT. S. W. B. DIEHL, JUDGE ADVOCATE GENERAL. July 1904 - Dec. 1907. Folded papers. 7 in. Unarranged.   21
  Chiefly unnumbered papers marked "Personal File." They appear to be confidential rather than personal; they relate chiefly to matters of discipline.

GENERAL FILE. Jan. 1905 - Mar. 1908. Folded papers. 133 ft. Arranged numerically, 1-9722. Registered in Entry 23; indexed in Entry 24.   22
  Letters received folded with press or carbon copies of letters sent. The numbers were assigned serially. One number usually applies only to a letter received and a copy of the letter sent in reply, or to a single letter. Sometimes several letters are filed under one number, but apparently all the numbers designate correspondents rather than subjects. Some letters with numbers belonging to this file are filed separately in Entries 88, 89, and 92. The file was discontinued on Mar. 31, 1908, after which date the general correspondence of the Judge Advocate General was filed with that of the Secretary's Office; but a few letters of date as late as June 1909 were added to the present file.

REGISTER OF THE GENERAL FILE. 1905-8. Cards 3 1/4 x 8 in. 10 ft. Arranged numerically, 1-9722.   23
  "History cards," giving date, writer, number, and abstract of each letter.

INDEX TO THE GENERAL FILE. 1905-8. Cards 3 1/4 x 8 in. 14 ft. 7 in. Arranged alphabetically by subjects and by correspondents' names or titles (1 alphabet).   24
  Gives file number and abstract for each entry, but not date.

LETTERS SENT BY THE SOLICITOR OF THE NAVY. June 1908 - Dec. 1911. 5 vols. 6 1/2 in. Press copies. Arranged chronologically.   25
  Opinions on matters of law and finance; endorsements on contracts and bonds; announcements of approval of contracts and bonds; requests for detail of officers on boards to report on final trials of vessels; letters relating to naval real estate; and orders for stationery and miscellaneous supplies.

LETTERS SENT BY TRISTAM B. JOHNSON, SOLICITOR OF THE NAVY. Apr.-July 1911. 1 vol. 1 in. Press copies. Arranged chronologically. Indexed.   26

B. Personnel Records, 1841-1943

More than half of the records of the Office of the Judge Advocate General pertain to the trial and punishment of officers and enlisted men of the Navy and the Marine Corps and to the promotion and retirement of Naval and Marine officers, with related registers, indexes, and correspondence.

The largest part of such records consists of reports from or records of proceedings of eleven types of courts and boards: general courts martial, summary courts martial, courts of inquiry, deck courts, boards of investigation, boards of inquest, naval examining boards, naval retiring boards, marine examining boards, marine retiring boards, and boards of medical examiners. The appointment, procedure, duties, and record-keeping of such courts and boards were governed by precise rules, the interpretation of which was a duty of the Judge Advocate General. The record of proceedings of a court or board normally included minutes of its sittings and transcripts of testimony, with originals or copies of precepts and letters of dissolution, documents introduced as evidence (exhibits), and other appended matter. When the work of a court or board was completed, the official record of its proceedings was forwarded to the Judge Advocate General (before 1880 to the Secretary of the Navy). Records of summary courts martial and deck courts were retained by the Office of the Judge Advocate General. Those of boards of medical examiners were forwarded to the Bureau of Medicine and Surgery and became part of its records. Those of other courts and boards were transmitted by the Judge Advocate General, with his endorsement, to the Secretary of the Navy and by him (in some cases) to the President for approval and were returned with the endorsements of these officials. Records retained by or returned to the Office of the Judge Advocate General were there assembled in numbered series as records of that Office.

Records of proceedings of courts and boards of different types have at times been combined in single series and at times been separated into several series. Records of proceedings of general courts martial, courts of inquiry, boards of investigation, and boards of inquest were in general bound together as a single series from June 1799 till April 1864, when records of general courts martial began to be bound in separate volumes. Records of proceedings of summary courts martial have been filed separately since such courts were first established by act of Congress, March 2, 1855, though all but the most recent of these records have been destroyed. Records of proceedings of naval and marine examining boards have apparently been filed together since 1861, when procedure for such boards was formally instituted. Records of proceedings of naval and marine retiring boards were filed separately from August 1861 till April 1871, and thereafter were combined. Records of proceedings of deck courts have been filed separately since such courts were first authorized in February 1909. Reports of boards of medical examiners have been part of the records of proceedings of all boards and courts of which the duties included that of ascertaining the physical condition of naval or marine personnel, but (as already mentioned) the records of proceedings of boards of medical examiners are usually filed by the Bureau of Medicine and Surgery.

1. Records Relating to General Courts Martial, Courts of Inquiry,
Boards of Investigation, and Boards of Inquest, 1841-1943

[Records of Proceedings of General Courts Martial, Courts of Inquiry,
Boards of Investigation, and Boards of Inquest. June 1799 - Nov. 1867.
156 vols. NRC 294.]

RECORDS OF PROCEEDINGS OF GENERAL COURTS MARTIAL. Feb. 1866 - Nov. 1940.
459 vols., ca. 1869 looseleaf binders, folded and flat papers, and
various other materials. 794 ft. Arranged numerically (volumes
and binders numbered, with gaps explained below, from 153 through
2835, cases therein from 4224 through 79074). Registered in
Entries 28 and 41; indexed in Entry 33.   27
Continuation of the preceding, which contains vols. 1-152, 172-173,
178, and 189. Each dossier, when complete, contains the precept appointing the court, letters detailing or detaching its several members, a
letter dissolving the court, the charges and specifications of charges,
minutes of the court consisting chiefly of a verbatim transcript of testimony, the plea of the defendant (often printed), copies of correspondence introduced as part of the minutes, the finding of the court, the
sentence in case of a finding of guilty, the endorsements of the Judge
Advocate General (beginning in 1880), the Secretary of the Navy, and the
President, and documents introduced in evidence and collected in an appendix, often being designated by numbers or letters by which they are
referred to in the minutes. All matter except the appendix is normally
transcribed on legal-size sheets, bound at the top. The exhibits, particularly those written on both sides or those that form pamphlets, bound
in the backs of the same volumes, may be made almost inaccessible by this method
of binding, and are often assembled in no definite order, either that of
their letters or numbers or any other. The unbound records are exhibits
that consist of bulky paper records or fragments and articles of metal,
glass, wood, cloth, and other substances--knives, bottles, blood-stained
garments, pistols, and a variety of other exhibits. The later records
have the following printed title page or one closely equivalent: "Record
of Proceedings of a General Court-Martial Convened [place inserted] by
Order of the Secretary of the Navy." Before vol. 840 (1910) a single
series of volume numbers was applied to records of proceedings of both general courts martial and courts of inquiry, which began to be bound apart
from each other in separate volumes with vol. 158 in Apr. 1864 but may have
been shelved together till 1910. During this period a volume number ap-
pearing on a volume of proceedings of one series would be lacking from the
other series. Certain volume numbers are lacking from both series, including vols. 246-354 (1878-79), 358-359, 363-365, 369-372, 376-377, 379, 386-
388, 391-392, 394-395, and various higher numbers. These gaps do not mark
gaps in the sequence of case numbers. Before vol. 360 (1879) all case
numbers are accounted for in one series or the other, and beginning with
that volume each series has case numbers that independently continue those
in vol. 357, each number thereafter designating a different case in each
series. In other words, no case numbers of either series are lacking. The
volumes that bore the missing numbers were not records of retiring boards,
which survive in their original bindings and are not numbered. They may
have been records of summary courts martial (since destroyed) or of naval
examining boards (since dismantled). These two classes of records, begun

in 1855 and 1861 respectively, do not fit a hypothesis calling for a
series that began in 1878 or 1879; but possibly one or both of these
classes were retained as loose papers till that time and were then bound
with numbers belonging to the sequence of volume numbers begun in 1799.
All general courts martial from 1861 to 1904 are registered and indexed,
with defendants' names and case numbers, in Entry 28. No index containing both names and case numbers is available in the National Archives
for the records subsequent to June 1904. Correspondence relating to
general court-martial cases and not bound in the records of proceedings,
Apr. 1908 - Aug. 1926, is included in the general file of the Office of
the Secretary of the Navy, chiefly under no. 26251 (1,139 trays, 136 cu.
ft., indexed in Entry 78), with subnumbers unrelated to the case numbers.

REGISTER OF GENERAL COURTS MARTIAL. Nov. 1861 - June 1904. 11 vols.
    2 ft. 8 in. Arranged chronologically. Indexed.   28
    Entries on a printed form, giving case number, date and place of trial,
charges, substance of specifications, plea, finding, sentence, and remarks
as to approval of sentence. Vols. 1-7 are labeled "Courts Martial," vols.
8-11 "General Courts Martial." Vol. 1 begins with no. 3102; vol. 11 ends
with no. 12061. See Entry 1 and NRC 295 and 296 for earlier indexes and
a register.

RECORDS OF PROCEEDINGS OF INVESTIGATORS AND BOARDS OF INVESTIGATION
    CONSIDERING CHARGES AGAINST CIVIL EMPLOYEES IN NAVY YARDS ("Navy
    Yard Cases"). Mar. 1841 - Feb. 1881. 6 vols. 1 ft. 5 in. Ar-
    ranged numerically, 1-29. Indexed.   29
    Some of the volumes are stained by dampness. The records of these
29 cases, consisting of reports or minutes, with orders and appended
exhibits, might have been included in the series described in Entry 30,
but for some reason were kept separate. They are listed in Appendix B.

RECORDS OF PROCEEDINGS OF COURTS OF INQUIRY, BOARDS OF INVESTIGATION,
    AND BOARDS OF INQUEST. May 1866 - Dec. 1940. 97 vols. and ca.
    968 looseleaf binders. 347 ft. Arranged numerically from case
    4398 through case 21330, with gaps explained below. Registered
    in Entry 31.   30
    The series begins with vols. 158-165, starting in Apr. 1864 with case
4300, in the Naval Records Collection (NRC 294). The first 35 vols.
(vols. 158-435, the gaps in this numbering being filled in part by volumes in Entry 27) are also numbered from I through XXXV. The case numbers
dovetail with those in Entry 27 through vol. 188 (ending with case 4716)
and are continuous in and after vol. 360 (beginning with case 4717). Volume numbers are scattered as far as vol. 778 (1902), are continuous for
vols. 809-878 (numbers also used for volumes of Entry 27), and are discontinued thereafter. The volumes through vol. 831 are labeled "Court-
Martial Records, Courts of Inquiry," vols. 832-878 are labeled "Courts of
Inquiry and Boards of Investigation," and the remaining binders are not
labeled except for case numbers. Cases previous to case 4300 are bound
in the same volumes with general court-martial cases. A record of proceedings of a court of inquiry, board of investigation, or board of inquest normally contains most of the classes of items included in the record
of proceedings of a general court martial, with the exception of a sentence.

REGISTER OF COURTS OF INQUIRY, BOARDS OF INVESTIGATION, AND BOARDS OF
INQUEST ("Courts of Inquire, No. 1"). Nov. 1861 - Mar. 1917.
1 vol. 3 in. Arranged numerically, 3101-6787. Indexed.   31
Gives case number, names of members of court, place and date of convening, subject before court, name of person concerned, and finding.
After case 5216 (Apr. 1910) the membership of the court is not given.
The earliest cases referred to in the register are bound with general
court-martial cases. The register was succeeded by cards labeled "Bound
Courts of Inquiry" in the index to the general file of the Office of
the Secretary of the Navy, 1897-1926; the cards begin with case 6788 and
end in June 1926 with case 14067.

REGISTER OF PRISONERS UNDER SENTENCE OF GENERAL COURT MARTIAL ("Court
Martial Prisoners"). Jan. 1877 - June 1892. 1 vol. 2 in. Ar-
ranged by place of imprisonment (prisons at Boston, Portsmouth,
New York, Wethersfield [State Prison, Connecticut], Norfolk, and
Mare Island, and prison ships of various foreign stations), there-
under chronologically. Indexed.   32
Gives name and rate of prisoner, dates of beginning and expiration
of confinement, place of confinement, and remarks.

LIST OF OFFICERS TRIED BY GENERAL COURT MARTIAL. 1879-1920. 1 looseleaf binder. 2 1/2 in.   33
(a) Alphabetical list of defendants, giving name and rank of each,
charges for which tried (designated by symbols), sentence imposed by
court (designated by number, 1-18, the significations of the numbers
being listed in the front of the binder), and action taken by reviewing authority; and (b) alphabetical list of offenses, with names of officers convicted of each entered chronologically thereunder, giving
rank, general court-martial order number, date of order, and volume of
"general court-martial order book" in which it is entered. The book
referred to is not known to be in the National Archives.

RECORDS RELATING TO AN INVESTIGATION OF THE NORFOLK NAVY YARD ("Com-
modore Mayo's Papers"). 1883-85. Folded papers. 1 ft. Un-
arranged.   34
The investigation resulted from charges made by the Hon. John D.
Dezendorf against Commo. William K. Mayo, Commandant, Naval Constructor
William H. Varney, and other officers of the Norfolk Navy Yard.

LETTERS SENT BY GENERAL COURTS MARTIAL IN THE CASES OF MEDICAL DIRECTOR
PHILIP S. WALES AND PAYMASTER GENERAL JOSEPH A. SMITH. Mar. 6 -
Oct. 22, 1885. 1 vol. 1 in. Press copies. Arranged chronolog-
ically.   35
In the first case the Judge Advocate was Lt. Samuel C. Lemly and the
President of the Court R. A. Ernest Simpson. In the second the Judge
Advocate was Paymaster Robert W. Allen, later Lieutenant Lemly, and the
President Commo. W. W. Queen.

GENERAL COURT-MARTIAL ORDERS. Jan. 1886 - Jan. 1889, Jan. 1891 - July
1892. 2 adhesive binders (numbered "2" and "4"). 4 1/2 in.
Printed. Arranged by calendar years, thereunder by serial
numbers.   36

Promulgations of action of general courts martial, giving place and date of holding of court, president of court, name of defendant, charges, finding, sentence, and approval of sentence.

RECORD OF AN INVESTIGATION INTO AFFAIRS AT THE NEW YORK NAVY YARD. 1888.
2 looseleaf binders. 8 in.   37
Report to the Secretary of the Navy, Nov. 22, 1888, by the investigators, Robert W. Allen, Paymaster, and J. Monroe Heiskell, Special Examiner, Department of Justice, including a record of proceedings undertaken in obedience to orders dated July 13 and 14, 1888.

RECORDS RELATING TO INVESTIGATIONS OF VARIOUS NAVY YARDS. 1894-98.
Envelopes and loose papers. 1 ft.   38
These papers seem to have been only partly arranged when most of them were filed in envelopes with penciled labels. They include (a) reports of investigations of the New York Navy Yard by Lt. John J. Knapp, Sept. 14, 1894, and Mar. 14, 1895, intermingled with records of a board of investigation of which Lt. N. T. Houston was Senior Member, June 1895, and records of an investigation by Comdr. C. H. Davis, July 1897 (loose papers in 1 tray); (b) fragmentary records of a board of investigation at New York appointed Dec. 27, 1895, of which Commo. R. L. Phythian was Senior Member and Lieutenant Knapp was recorder, with fragments of an earlier report by the latter (1 envelope); (c) report by Lieutenant Knapp of an investigation at the Boston Navy Yard, Sept. 14, 1895 (1 envelope); (d) fragmentary records of investigations of the League Island and Norfolk Navy Yards by Theodore Roosevelt, Assistant Secretary of the Navy, May 1897 (2 envelopes); (e) report of investigation of the Washington Navy Yard by Lt. H. L. Draper, Mar. 1898 (1 stapled volume); (f) fragmentary records of an investigation of the Philadelphia Navy Yard by Lieutenant Knapp, Sept. 1898 (1 envelope); and (g) report of investigation of the Norfolk Navy Yard by Lieutenant Knapp, Oct. 18, 1898.

RECORD OF THE PROCEEDINGS OF AN INVESTIGATION OF THE NEW YORK NAVY YARD.
June 24 - July 13, 1897. 4 vols. (original and duplicate). 8 in.   39
The object of investigation, made by Comdr. Charles H. Davis, was the methods of Naval Constructor Francis T. Bowles in employing and retaining men.

RECORD OF THE PROCEEDINGS OF AN INVESTIGATION OF THE MARE ISLAND NAVY YARD. Nov. 19 - Dec. 8, 1897. 2 vols. 4 in.   40
Investigation, by Lt. John J. Knapp, of alleged discriminations against veterans of the Civil War.

REGISTER OF GENERAL COURTS MARTIAL. July 1909 - June 1943. 32 vols.
3 ft. 4 in. Arranged by fiscal years, thereunder chiefly by naval districts, thereunder chronologically.   41
Gives date when case went to court, file number of report on which charges and specifications were founded (chiefly under no. 26251 of the general file of the Secretary's Office), name of defendant, rank or rate, date when record was received (basis of the chronological arrangement), consecutive case number, finding of court, sentence as approved, and date of approval. First 22 vols. labeled "G. C. M."; last 10 vols., "G. C. M. Record Book."

RECORDS OF PROCEEDINGS OF GENERAL COURTS MARTIAL FOR PERSONNEL OF THE
COAST GUARD. Apr. 1917 - Aug. 1919. 7 looseleaf binders. 2 ft.
5 in. Arranged by serial numbers of cases, 1-173.   42
Similar in contents to Entry 27.

OPINIONS ISSUED BY THE JUDGE ADVOCATE GENERAL ON MATTERS OF LAW AND
PROCEDURE IN GENERAL COURTS MARTIAL ("Opinions, G. C. M. Review
Desk"). Mar. 1920 - June 1922. 1 looseleaf binder. 2 in.
Carbon copies.   43
Chiefly copies of endorsements by the Judge Advocate General on records of general courts martial, arranged alphabetically under the following subject headings: accused, adjournment, argument, assault, breaking
arrest, challenge, charges and specifications, check, clemency, confes-
sions, desertion, embezzlement, errors and irregularities, evidence,
findings and evidence, jurisdiction, miscellaneous, offense, principle,
procedure, revision, and theft.

ROUGH REGISTER OF GENERAL COURTS MARTIAL ("Record"). Sept. 1924 - Jan.
1935. 3 vols. 4 in. Arranged numerically.   44
Gives number, defendant's name, rating, charges, finding, sentence
of court, sentence as approved, statement made on stand, age of defendant,
date of enlistment, and dates of sending charges and specifications, of
receipt of case, of referral to Bureau of Navigation or Commandant of
Marine Corps, of transmission to Secretary of Navy, of approval by Secretary, and of promulgation. Some of these items of information are not
uniformly given. In the first volume (Sept. 1924 - Aug. 1926) the numbers
are subnumbers under no. 26251 of the general file, referring to serial
numbers of recommendations for general courts martial; in the other volumes the numbers are consecutive case numbers. In all 3 vols. the entries
are nearly illegible.

LETTERS FROM THE SECRETARY OF THE NAVY INDICATING HIS ACTION WITH RESPECT
TO RECORDS OF GENERAL COURTS MARTIAL. Jan.-Dec. 1925. 1 looseleaf binder. 3 in. Arranged chronologically.   45

ANNOUNCEMENTS OF CONVICTIONS BY GENERAL COURTS MARTIAL ("Promulgated
Letters"). Jan.-Dec. 1929, Jan. 1931 - Dec. 1943. 16 looseleaf
binders. 3 ft. 9 in. Carbon copies. Arranged chronologically. 46
Circular letters, each stamped "promulgating letter," giving name of
defendant, date and place of trial, charges, and sentence. A binder for
1930 is lacking.

2. Records Relating to Summary Courts Martial and Deck Courts,
1855-1930

INDEX TO SUMMARY COURTS MARTIAL. Apr. 1855 - June 1880, Jan. 1886 - Jan.
1895. 5 vols. 6 in. Arranged chronologically by volumes, thereunder by first letter of defendants' names, thereunder chronologically.   47
Gives defendant's name and rating, date and number of trial, and yard
at or vessel on which it was held. The first volume begins with case 1578

on Apr. 25, 1855; the cases with lower numbers are not found. The last
volume closes with case 20586. Vols. 1-3 and 6 (Apr. 1855 - June 1880,
Apr. 1893 - Jan. 1895) are labeled "Index to Summary Court-Martial Files."
The index from Jan. 1886 to Apr. 1893, "Summary Courts Martial Received,"
lacks a volume number, is of smaller dimensions than the other volumes,
and gives the date of receipt of each case, defendant's name and rating,
and case number. Like the other volumes, it is arranged alphabetically
by first letter. If it is not actually vol. 5 of the series, it may
serve as a substitute. Vol. 4 is missing.

REGISTER OF SUMMARY COURTS MARTIAL ("Record of Summary Courts Martial").
    July 1880 - Sept. 1887. 2 vols. 5 in. Arranged by serial number
    of cases, 13120-16063. Indexed.   48
    Entries on a printed form, giving case number, place where court was
held, defendant's name and rating, by whose order tried, substance of
charges, finding, sentence, and remarks. The latter part of the second
volume is blank, suggesting that this record was discontinued. No
similar record of earlier date is found. Since the records of proceedings of summary courts martial have been destroyed, no information concerning charges and sentences before 1880 is available except as it may
be incidentally included in other series of records.

INDEX TO SUMMARY COURTS MARTIAL ("Record of Summary Courts Martial").
    Jan. 1895 - Sept. 1904. 4 vols. 8 in. Arranged chronologi-
    cally by volumes, thereunder by first letter of defendants'
    names, thereunder chronologically.   49
    Gives date when case was received, defendant's name, rating, case
number, place and date of trial, offense, sentence, action, and remarks.
The first 2 vols. are not numbered; the others, numbered 3 and 4, are
externally of the same format as the 2 vols. of Entry 48. For the period
between the two series, as for that before 1880, no information concerning charges and sentences is available except as it may be found incidentally.

REGISTER OF SUMMARY COURT-MARTIAL CHECKAGES. Dec. 1902 - Mar. 1904,
    Mar. 1907 - Jan. 1909. 3 vols. 3 in. Arranged chronologically. 50
    Record of deductions from income of men convicted by summary courts
martial, made to discharge fines by installments. Gives date of check-
age, name of enlisted man, rate, station, and amount.

SLIP RECORD OF SUMMARY COURTS MARTIAL. Jan. 1904 - Dec. 1930. Slips
    3½ x 8 in. 144 ft. Arranged by calendar years, thereunder
    alphabetically by defendants' names.   51
    Gives defendant's name and rate, ship or station, date of trial, of-
fense, finding, and sentence. These summaries, prepared in the Office
of the Judge Advocate General, are the only form in which this information has been preserved.

REPORTS OF SUMMARY COURT-MARTIAL CHECKAGES. 1905-8. Folded papers.
    6 ft. 4 in. Arranged by years, thereunder alphabetically by
    defendants' names.   52
    Acknowledgments, from commanding officers, of notification of approvals
of summary court-martial sentences involving forfeit of pay.

SLIP RECORD OF DECK COURTS. Feb. 1909 - Dec. 1930. Slips $3\frac{1}{2}$ x 8 in.
140 ft. Arranged by calendar years, thereunder alphabetically
by defendants' names.   53
Give case number, defendant's name and rate, offense, record of
previous convictions, names of witnesses, plea, finding, sentence, and
commanding officer's approval. The slips in trays (1909-15) and those
in drawers (1912-30) overlap chronologically. Deck courts were authorized
by an act of Feb. 16, 1909; the first deck-court record was received by
the Office of the Judge Advocate General Mar. 11, 1909. These slips
were prepared in that Office, and the original records (except Entry 54)
were destroyed.

RECORDS OF PROCEEDINGS OF DECK COURTS. Jan.-Dec. 1910. 23 looseleaf
binders. 7 ft. 3 in. Arranged by serial number of cases, 1-
14137.   54
One sheet for each case, printed or mimeographed with entries on both
sides, giving charges, order for trial signed by commanding officer,
consent to be tried signed by defendant, date of enlistment, rate of pay
per month, previous convictions during current enlistment, names of
witnesses for prosecution, plea, finding, sentence, and approval of sentence by commanding officer. These are the only original records of
deck courts that are known to have been preserved.

3. Records Relating to Examining Boards and Retiring Boards,
1836-1941

REGISTER OF EXAMINATIONS OF REGULAR ENGINEERS. July 1836 - Apr. 1894.
1 vol. 2 in. Arranged in inverse order of rank (from third
assistant engineer to chief engineer), thereunder chronologically.   55
Data for third assistant engineers (Jan. 1842 - Feb. 1868), second
assistant engineers and assistant engineers (Nov. 1837 - after Oct.
1883), first assistant and passed assistant engineers (Nov. 1836 - Apr.
1894), and chief engineers (July 1836 - Mar. 1894). Gives name of
candidate, rank, grade for which examined, age, experience, subjects
in which examined, grades received, votes of examining board, average
of votes, and place and date of examination.

RECORDS OF PROCEEDINGS OF NAVAL AND MARINE RETIRING BOARDS ("Retiring
Boards"). Aug. 1861 - Aug. 1909. 54 vols. 18 ft. Arranged by
serial number of cases, 1-1089. Registered in Entry 59.   56
Precept appointing board, minutes of proceedings and verbatim transcript
of testimony, and endorsement by the Judge Advocate General, the Secretary
of the Navy, and the President, with appended report of a board of medical
examiners, record of candidate's service, and any documents introduced as
supporting papers--the whole with a printed cover sheet labeled "Record of
Proceedings of the Naval Retiring Board Convened [place inserted] in the
Case of [name inserted]," or the equivalent for a marine retiring board.
The record was filed even though the candidate was retained on the active
list. Records of proceedings of marine retiring boards were filed separately till 1871 (Entry 57). Procedure for retiring boards was established
by an act of Aug. 3, 1861. See Entries 62 and 65.

RECORDS OF PROCEEDINGS OF MARINE RETIRING BOARDS ("Marine Retiring
    Boards"). Nov. 1861 - Apr. 1871. 2 vols. 6 in. Arranged
    chronologically. Table of contents.   57
    Proceedings in the cases of 14 officers of the Marine Corps. Later
proceedings were bound with those of naval retiring boards (Entry 56).

RECORDS OF PROCEEDINGS OF NAVAL AND MARINE EXAMINING BOARDS. 1861 - ca.
    1903. Folders. 55 ft. Arranged alphabetically by candidates'
    names.   58
    Proceedings of boards to consider the promotion of officers, contain-
ing precept to board; notice to candidate; "Report on the Fitness of Officers" (a printed form received, after 1889, from the Bureau of Navigation,
containing information entered by the candidate and by his commanding officers); statements by candidate; report of a medical examining board;
endorsements of the Bureau of Medicine and Surgery, the Bureau of Navigation or the Commandant of the Marine Corps, the Judge Advocate General
(after 1880), and the President; and letter of transmittal from the Secretary of the Navy to the President, conveying the Secretary's endorsement
with the record. The record is provided with a printed cover sheet labeled
"Record of Proceedings of a Naval Examining Board Convened at [place in-
serted] in the Case of [candidate's name inserted]," or the equivalent for
a marine examining board. The cover sheet may bear penciled notations concerning the retirement, resignation, or death of a candidate. The records
bear evidence of having been formerly bound in volumes. No indication is
found of the number of volumes, their arrangement, whether they formed two
series (naval and marine) or only one, or when they were dismantled and
their contents stapled in folders.

[Report of the Naval Examining Board to Consider the Promotion of Certain
    Officers. May 26, 1879. 1 vol. NRC 298.]

REGISTER OF RETIRING BOARDS ("Record of Retiring Boards"). July 1880 -
    Apr. 1911. 1 vol. 3 in. Arranged by serial numbers of cases,
    240-1188. Indexed.   59
    Gives date and place of examination, name and rank of officer examined,
date of order for examination, and finding. The latter part of the volume is blank, suggesting that the record was not continued.

REGISTER OF EXAMINING BOARDS ("Record of Examining Boards"). Sept.
    1880 - Nov. 1904. 3 vols. 9 in. Arranged chronologically.
    Indexed.   60
    Gives date and place of examination, name and rank of officer examined,
date of order for examination, finding, and action taken on finding. The
latter part of vol. 3 is blank, suggesting that the record was not continued.

MEMORANDA FROM THE CHIEF OF THE BUREAU OF NAVIGATION ANNOUNCING OFFICERS
    ORDERED TO APPEAR BEFORE EXAMINING OR RETIRING BOARDS ("Officers
    Ordered to Examination"). Aug. 1890 - Feb. 1895, Oct. 1896 - May
    1900. 4 adhesive binders. 1 ft. Indexed.   61
    One binder is obviously lacking.

RECORDS OF PROCEEDINGS OF NAVAL AND MARINE EXAMINING BOARDS AND NAVAL
    AND MARINE RETIRING BOARDS. Ca. 1890-1941. Looseleaf binders
    and folders. 791 ft.   62

In contents this series is similar to Entries 56 and 58. The cases in binders (ca. 1890 – ca. 1933, in somewhat imperfect alphabetical order) and the cases in folders (ca. 1928 – 1941, alphabetical) overlap. No difference between the two groups of cases is detectable. Apparently some cases have been removed from the binders and stapled in folders. Precise dates for the beginning of the series and for the change in method of filing are not easily established.

REQUESTS FROM THE BUREAU OF NAVIGATION FOR RECORDS RELATING TO FITNESS
    OF OFFICERS. May 1935 – May 1937 (Nav. 325). Stapled volumes.
    1 ft. 3 in. Carbon copies. Arranged chronologically.   63

4. Other Personnel Records, 1860-1931

PERSONNEL REPORTS FROM COMMANDING OFFICERS. 1860-95. Folded papers.
    10 ft. 7 in. Unarranged.   64
    Reports of punishments of enlisted men on naval vessels and in shore establishments; lists of prisoners in naval prisons and prison ships; lists of staff and line officers; reports of attainment of officers; and reports of conduct of enlisted men. Of these classes of reports only the first two appear to be within the province of the Office of the Judge Advocate General. The others may have been transferred or referred to that Office because of some expected relevance to disciplinary matters. From 1862 to 1889 the reports of conduct of enlisted men would normally have been filed by the Bureau of Equipment and Recruiting, and the records relating to officers by the Office of Detail; and in 1889 these records would normally have been transferred to the Bureau of Navigation. In and after 1880, however, the records relating to officers are stamped by both the Office of Detail and the Office of the Judge Advocate General, though rarely given file numbers by the latter.

RECORDS OF PROCEEDINGS OF THREE BOARDS. Sept. 1861 – Apr. 1864, June
    1866, Aug. 1867. 1 looseleaf binder. 3½ in.   65
    (a) Record of proceedings (Sept. 16, 1861 – Apr. 4, 1864) of the Board appointed Sept. 16, 1861, in compliance with an act of Aug. 3, 1861, to consider the cases of officers incapacitated for active service, to determine whether their disabilities or incompetencies were incurred in line of duty, and, if not, to recommend whether they should be retired on furlough pay or wholly retired from the service. The Board was convened at New York, with Philip Hamilton as Judge Advocate and Capt. Hiram Paulding as President (the latter succeeded by R. A. George W. Storer Oct. 18, 1861, and by Commo. William Mervine Oct. 7, 1862). The record consists of minutes and copies of letters received and sent. Transcripts of testimony and the accompanying exhibits are in Entry 58. (b) Report submitted to the Commandant of the Philadelphia Navy Yard June 18, 1866 (and by him forwarded to the Secretary of the Navy June 26) by a board appointed by him, June 8, with Comdr. William H. Macomb as Senior Member, to investigate charges against certain officers of the Navy Yard. (c) Report submitted to the Commandant of the Boston Navy Yard Aug. 10, 1867, by a board appointed by him July 29, with William Johnson, Surgeon, as Senior Member, to investigate charges made by Capt. E. G. Parrott, commanding the USS Ohio, receiving ship at Boston,

against Paymaster McKean Buchanan, serving on the Ohio. Items (b) and (c) seem identical in character with those included in Entry 30, and have no relation to item (a) beyond that of juxtaposition.

LISTS OF OFFICERS DETAILED TO OR DETACHED FROM SERVICE ON BOARDS AND
     COURTS. Feb. 1876 - Mar. 1895. 6 adhesive binders. 1 ft. 4 in.
     Arranged chronologically. Indexed.   66
    Notices received from the Office of Detail, after 1889 from the Bureau of Navigation. Variously labeled "Bureau of Equipment and Recruiting," "Details for Courts &c.," "Detail," "Courts & Boards," and "Organization of Courts, Boards, etc."

LETTERS FROM COURTS AND BOARDS. Jan. 1880 - Dec. 1882. 5 vols. 1 ft.
     1 in. Arranged chronologically.   67
    Chiefly letters of transmittal for records of proceedings, with a few letters requesting copies of service records for use by courts and boards.

REGISTER OF ORDERS ESTABLISHING GENERAL COURTS MARTIAL, COURTS OF INQUIRY,
     EXAMINING BOARDS, AND RETIRING BOARDS. July 1880 - Oct. 1890.
     1 vol. $2\frac{1}{2}$ in. Arranged by type of board or court, thereunder
     chronologically.   68
    The orders were issued by the Secretary of the Navy.

CORRESPONDENCE RELATING TO DESERTION AND DISCHARGE ("Desertions").
     Oct. 1883 - July 1908. Folded papers. 20 ft. 7 in. Arranged
     chronologically, 1883-92, and numerically (2-D through 3198-D,
     with many numbers lacking), June 1892 - July 1908. Registered
     in Entry 72.   69
    The correspondence before 1892 (9 trays), bearing numbers belonging to the general file, consists largely of forms labeled "Application for Certificate in Lieu of Discharge" and "Application for Certificate of Honorable Service" (referred from the Bureau of Navigation), carbon copies of replies to applicants, and correspondence with the Bureau of Navigation, the Commissioner of Pensions, and the Fourth Auditor. Later correspondence contains some matter of similar character but consists largely of a form labeled "Application for Removal of Charge of Desertion," giving details of applicant's naval service and appointing an attorney to represent him, with a separate "descriptive list" to identify the applicant. Some of the correspondence relates to changes of name, correction of records, and revocation of dismissal. See Entry 71. Similar matter relating to Civil War desertions is in the general file of the Office of the Secretary of the Navy under no. 26539, beginning June 30, 1908.

ORDERS RELATING TO COURTS AND BOARDS ("Courts Martial, Courts of Inquiry,
     Examining Boards, Retiring Boards"). Oct. 1884 - Nov. 1886.
     2 vols. $5\frac{1}{2}$ in. Handwritten copies. Arranged chronologically.
     Indexed.   70
    Orders issued by the Secretary of the Navy and the Judge Advocate General appointing and dissolving courts and boards, transmitting charges and specifications to courts martial, transmitting testimonials and other documents to courts and boards, detailing and detaching

particular members, transmitting records of proceedings (with recommendations) to the President, announcing approval of sentences, and directing commanding officers to execute the sentences.

REPLIES TO APPEALS FOR REMOVAL OF THE CHARGE OF DESERTION. Jan. 1889 - Jan. 1896. 1 vol. 1½ in. Press copies. Arranged chronologically. Indexed.   71
    Two form letters, the first referring to an act of Aug. 14, 1888, "to relieve certain appointed or enlisted men of the Navy and Marine Corps from the charge of desertion," Jan. 22 - Oct. 31, 1889, and the second referring to an act of Apr. 14, 1890, "for the relief of soldiers and sailors who enlisted or served under assumed names, while minors or otherwise, in the Army or Navy, during the War of the Rebellion," Mar. 30, 1891 - Jan. 15, 1896. The letters give no information beyond announcing that an application has been received and will be considered and the Department's decision thereon will be given. See Entry 69.

INDEX TO CORRESPONDENCE RELATING TO DESERTION AND DISCHARGE ("Record of Miscellaneous Reports"). July 1892 - July 1908. 2 vols. 5 in. Arranged chronologically by volumes, thereunder by first letter of correspondents' names, thereunder chronologically.   72
    Gives file number (see Entry 69), correspondent's name, date of letter, subject, date of referral of letter to Bureau of Navigation and of return to Office of Judge Advocate General, action taken, and to whom reply was sent. Covers letters numbered from 3 through 3198.

MEMORANDA TO BUREAUS AND THE MARINE CORPS ANNOUNCING FINDINGS AND SENTENCES OF COURTS MARTIAL. Sept. 1892 - Dec. 1911. 130 vols. 15 ft. Press copies. Arranged chronologically. Indexed.   73
    Mainly to the Chief of the Bureau of Navigation and the Commandant of the Marine Corps. Vols. 1-57 are labeled "Memoranda to Bureaus and the Marine Corps"; vols. 58-135, "Memorandum Book." The volume numbers from 49 through 79 are not entirely legible; they do not correspond to the chronological order of the volumes; and they allow for five numbers more than the number of volumes.

LETTERS SENT RELATING TO COURTS MARTIAL ("Courts Martial," later "Courts"). Dec. 1898 - Dec. 1911. 302 vols. 33 ft. Press copies. Arranged chronologically. Indexed.   74
    Orders to judge advocates transmitting charges and specifications of charges (often including copies of these) or returning cases for revision; orders to commandants and commanding officers of ships relative to prisoners sentenced by courts martial; endorsements; and occasional letters to Congressmen and others concerning courts martial. After Mar. 1908 most of the letters are under nos. 26251, 26262, and 26267 of the general file of the Office of the Secretary of the Navy. Many of the letters are signed by the Secretary of the Navy.

CORRESPONDENCE RELATING TO THE APPOINTMENT AND DISSOLUTION OF BOARDS AND COURTS. May 1903 - Jan. 1911. Envelopes and folded papers. 6 ft. Arranged chronologically.   75
    In two groups, numbered with gaps from 1-M through 857-M (envelopes) and from 154-M through 1001-M (folded papers), which apparently form a

single series relating to membership of general courts martial, courts of inquiry, examining boards, retiring boards, and boards of investigation. The records consist chiefly of memoranda from the Bureau of Navigation requesting the appointment or detachment of particular officers as members, and press copies of letters of appointment and detachment sent by the Judge Advocate General to officers. Why the groups were not interfiled is not clear.

REGISTER OF PROBATIONERS ("Record"). Sept. 1906 - Nov. 1909. 1 vol. 1¼ in. Arranged numerically, 1-329.   <u>76</u>
    Gives name and rate of probationer, dates of commencement and expiration of probation, length of term imposed, and final disposition of case (unconditional restoration to duty, desertion, requirement to serve sentence, or miscellaneous).

LISTS OF PRISONERS CONFINED IN SHIPS AND SHORE ESTABLISHMENTS. Oct. 1906 - Dec. 1930. Folded and flat papers. 4 ft. Unarranged.   <u>77</u>
    Weekly lists from commanding officers, indicating name and rate of prisoner, date of reception in prison, and date of release, 1908-30; and monthly lists giving name and rate, conduct average (expressed as a grade), and date of expiration of confinement, Oct. 1906 - Oct. 1907.

INDEXES TO CORRESPONDENCE RELATING TO COURTS MARTIAL, DECK COURTS, AND PROVOST COURTS. 1908-26. Cards 3¼ x 8 in. 56 ft.   <u>78</u>
    The correspondence covered by these indexes is part of the general file of the Office of the Secretary of the Navy but relates almost exclusively to business of the Judge Advocate General, by whose Office the indexes were evidently prepared. They refer to the following: (1) Courts martial and deck courts for Navy and Marine Corps personnel, chiefly under nos. 26251 (recommendations for trial by general court martial, beginning Apr. 1908), 26262 (general court-martial records from stations, beginning Feb. 1908), 26287 (miscellaneous matter pertaining to summary courts martial, beginning Mar. 1908), 27217 (deck courts, beginning Dec. 1908), and 27228 (letters in behalf of men whose cases have not been received, beginning July 1909). Under these numbers and others each man's case is assigned a different subnumber. The indexes do not refer to records of proceedings of courts or give case numbers of such records. They are in two alphabets, one for general courts martial, the other for summary courts martial and deck courts. (2) Provost courts in Haiti and the Dominican Republic, Mar. 1916 - Apr. 1926, chiefly under nos. 5526-39 and 16870-47 (1 ft. 7 in.). (3) Courts martial and deck courts for personnel of the Coast Guard, Apr. 1917 - May 1926, under no. 28762 (6 in.).

PRECEPTS ISSUED TO MEMBERS OF BOARDS. July-Dec. 1909. 1 vol. 1¼ in. Press copies. Arranged chronologically. Indexed.   <u>79</u>

RECORD OF JUDGE ADVOCATES AND COUNSEL IN IMPORTANT COURT-MARTIAL CASES, AND LIST OF OFFICERS HAVING LEGAL TRAINING OR EXPERIENCE. July 1911 - Aug. 1916. 1 vol. 2 in.   <u>80</u>
    Index to p. 1-3 (subject and name); "Specific Cases," giving name of judge advocate, counsel, case, case number, charge, and date and place of trial, July 1911 - Aug. 1916; and "General List," alphabetical, of

names and ranks of officers, followed by unexplained symbols.

LETTERS RECEIVED RELATING TO PROPOSED CHANGES IN ARTICLE 4893 OF THE
     NAVAL REGULATIONS, CONCERNING ABSENCE WITHOUT LEAVE. Jan.-Aug.
     1914. Loose papers. 2 in. Unarranged.   81

   In reply to a letter of the Secretary of the Navy, Jan. 13, 1914;
received by the Bureau of Navigation and stamped with no. 794-335, belonging to its general file, but apparently transmitted to and filed by
the Judge Advocate General. The general file of the Bureau of Navigation contains under this number various replies to a letter of the Chief
of that Bureau dated Sept. 11, 1916, giving opinions on proposed measures
to control leave-breaking; but the file contains no reference to the ex-
istence of earlier correspondence under the same number and not stapled
in the folder, which contains not only 794-335 but lower and higher
numbers.

RECORD OF WAR PRISONERS (Form AGO 597). 1917-18. Cards 3 3/4 x 8 1/2
     in. 7 1/2 in. Arranged alphabetically by prisoners' names.   82

   Gives prisoner's name and number, where and when captured, rank or
occupation, sex, nationality, age, height, complexion, color of eyes and
hair, place of birth, home address, name and address of person to be
notified in case of emergency, and medical record. It is not clear
whether the prisoners were naval prisoners or under what circumstances
the cards were transferred from the War Department.

LETTERS SENT RELATING TO COURTS MARTIAL. Aug. 1929 - Dec. 1931.
     2 looseleaf binders. 6 in. Carbon copies. Arranged chronologi-
     cally.   83

   First binder (Aug.-Nov. 1929) unlabeled; second labeled "Copies of
Letters & Despatches, Section B, Office of J. A. G., Navy Department,"
and designated as vol. 1. Both contain copies of precepts to courts
martial, appointments and detachments of officers to serve on such
courts, endorsements, orders relating to prisoners convicted by courts
martial, and similar letters.

C. Financial Records, 1869-1943

   The records described below pertain to legal questions affecting the
interrelated subjects of naval contracts, naval real estate, and claims
against the Navy Department. The records concern only incidentally the
receipt and disbursement of public funds (of which the general supervision
was retained by the Office of the Secretary of the Navy), the administration of naval real estate (under the direction of the Bureau of Yards and
Docks), or the settlement of claims that involved no probability of legal
contest. The Office of the Judge Advocate General was the custodian of
leases, releases, and similar legal instruments, of documents presented or
collected in connection with claims and litigation, and of contracts made
by the Navy Department (department contracts) as distinguished from supply
contracts (made by the Bureau of Supplies and Accounts for all units of the
Navy and the Department) and from contracts made by particular bureaus for
their own purposes.

From July 1908 to September 1921, as explained in the introduction to this checklist, all these matters were handled by the Office of the Solicitor of the Navy, which was of coordinate authority and status with the Office of the Judge Advocate General, the latter being concerned during this period only with legal matters relating to personnel of the Navy and the Marine Corps. In a sense, therefore, a large part of the records here described originated as records of the Office of the Solicitor. That Office, however, received only functions formerly handled by the Office of the Judge Advocate General, by which, after thirteen years, it was absorbed; and in consequence many series begun by one Office were continued by the other, before and after 1908 and 1921. It would be inconvenient and unprofitable to list the records of the two Offices separately, and no effort is made to do so.

CONTRACTS AND RELATED CORRESPONDENCE ("Contracts"). Sept. 1869 – Dec.
    1886. 1 vol. 3 in. Arranged chronologically. Indexed.   <u>84</u>
  Copies of contracts, Sept. 1869 – Dec. 1885, and of correspondence, Mar. 1880 – Dec. 1886. The purpose and origin of the volume are not clear, and there is no indication of the reason why most contracts made by the Department during these years were omitted.

MEMORANDA RELATIVE TO CLAIMS PRESENTED UNDER THE DEFICIENCY ACT OF JUNE
    14, 1878. June 1878 – June 1880. 1 vol. 2 in. Arranged chrono-
    logically. Indexed.   <u>85</u>
  The act of June 14, 1878, appropriated $765,592.12 to discharge unpaid obligations of the Navy Department. These had been a subject of Congressional inquiry. The volume consists chiefly of notes dated and signed by the Secretary of the Navy, apparently for his own guidance in relations with Congress.

ABSTRACTS OF CONTRACTS. July 1883 – Apr. 1885. 1 adhesive binder.
    $2\frac{1}{2}$ in. Arranged chronologically. Indexed.   <u>86</u>
  Apparently working papers.

DEPARTMENT CONTRACTS AND BONDS ("Contracts"). May 1886 – Aug. 1893.
    5 vols. (numbered 8-12). 1 ft. 3 in. Arranged chronologically.
    Indexed.   <u>87</u>
  A similar series, 1794-1842, is in the Naval Records Collection (NRC 235). Other volumes of the same kind, including vols. 1-7 of the present series, must have been maintained between 1842 and 1886; but nothing is known of their whereabouts.

CORRESPONDENCE AND DATA CONCERNING LEGAL QUESTIONS AFFECTING NAVAL
    VESSELS. Ca. 1887 – ca. 1906. Folded papers. 175 ft. Arranged
    by the numbers of the boxes in which the records were received by
    the National Archives, thereunder by ships' names.   <u>88</u>
  Chiefly numbered letters segregated from the general file and relating to fulfillment of contracts with shipbuilders and with manufacturers of ship machinery and equipment. The distribution of the records in boxes had no obvious significance.

CORRESPONDENCE AND DATA CONCERNING BIDS, BONDS, CONTRACTS, AND PROPOSALS. 1888-1907. Folded papers. 7 ft. 10 in. Unarranged.   **89**
    Chiefly numbered letters segregated from the general file, having no apparent community of subject beyond that indicated by the title.

SPECIFICATIONS. Ca. 1888 - ca. 1922. Ca. 370 vols. 32 ft. Printed. Unarranged.   **90**
    File copies, each signed by a representative of a contracting firm and a representative of the Navy Department (frequently the Secretary of the Navy). Stamped with numbers belonging to the general files, indicating that the volumes were enclosures to correspondence. They are filed with records of the Office of the Judge Advocate General, probably because they were regarded as parts of the texts of contracts.

PAPERS RELATING TO THE ENLARGEMENT OF THE UNITED STATES NAVAL ACADEMY. 1895-1915. Folded papers, folders, envelopes, blueprints, and 6 bound vols. 3 ft. 6 in. Unarranged.   **91**
    Records assembled in connection with claims submitted by the Noel Construction Company, the Hoffman Engineering and Construction Company, and others, consisting of correspondence, proposals, specifications, copies of contracts, blueprints, miscellaneous publications, and the following manuscript volumes: register of bills approved under appropriations for the Naval Academy, July 1895 - Sept. 1903, maintained by the Bureau of Navigation; register of expenditures on Naval Academy buildings, Apr. 1902 - Oct. 1905 (no. 5474 of the general file of the Office of the Secretary of the Navy); press copies of vouchers paid from the appropriation Buildings and Grounds, Naval Academy, Sept. 1908 - Sept. 1908 (3 vols.); and register of vouchers paid from the same appropriation, Oct. 1905 - Dec. 1906.

CORRESPONDENCE RELATING TO CLAIMS. 1903-7. Folded papers. 7½ in. Unarranged.   **92**
    The papers, all with numbers belonging to the general files, have apparently nothing in common except that they relate to claims, particularly those resulting from collisions.

LETTERS SENT RELATING TO CONTRACTS ("Contracts"). Apr. 1909 - Dec. 1911. 13 vols. 1 ft. 4 in. Press copies. Arranged chronologically. Indexed.   **93**
    From the Assistant Secretary of the Navy and the Solicitor, authorizing changes in contracts, approving proposed contracts, approving or acknowledging payment of bills, interpreting clauses of contracts, appointing boards to examine fulfillment of contracts, requiring payment of penalties or damages, or otherwise concerning contracts.

RECORDS RELATING TO PROPOSALS AND CONTRACTS FOR SHIPS. 1910-16. Envelopes, folders, blueprints, and pamphlets. 3 ft. 4 in. Unarranged.   **94**

CORRESPONDENCE, BRIEFS, MEMORANDA, AND NOTES OF THE SOLICITOR OF THE NAVY CONCERNING THE PEARL HARBOR DRY DOCK. May 1913 - Nov. 1914. 4 envelopes. 3 in. Unarranged   **95**
Fragmentary records relative to fulfillment of one or more contracts.

RECORDS RELATING TO FORMER NAVAL PROPERTIES. Ca. 1914 - ca. 1941.
Envelopes and folders. 5 ft. 10 in. Arranged alphabetically
by States, Territories, and insular possessions (1 alphabet),
thereunder alphabetically by sites of properties.   96
    Chiefly correspondence relating to the sale or other disposition of
naval real estate, with photographs, blueprints, abstracts of title,
and copies of leases, permits, releases, and other instruments. The
file contains papers as early as Jan. 1914 and as late as Feb. 1941;
most of the papers are subsequent to 1925.

RECORDS RELATING TO SHIP REPAIR. 1915-25. Folders. 2 ft. 1 in. Arranged alphabetically by contractors' names, with 1 tray of
miscellaneous papers at the end. Penciled list of contractors
in first tray.   97
    Copies of department contracts, cancellations, and releases, with
attached correspondence.

COMPILATION OF LAWS AND REGULATIONS RELATING TO NAVAL PROPERTY. Ca.
1916-26. Cards 6 x 4 in. 7 in. Arranged alphabetically by
general subjects.   98
    Quotations from and citations of decisions of the Supreme Court, acts
of Congress, opinions and decisions of the Attorney General and the
Judge Advocate General, decisions of the Secretary of the Navy, and other
sources, on such matters as contracts, easements, damages, eminent domain,
rent, claims, licenses, prizes, abstracts of title, attorneys' fees, and
acts of God. The drawer is labeled "Permits Acquired & Permits Granted,"
but the label has no relation to the contents of the drawer. The latest
date in the cards is Aug. 1926; most of the citations were apparently
made in or about 1916; but some are to decisions and documents as early as
1804.

SURETY BONDS OF ENLISTED MEN OR NAVAL EMPLOYEES RECEIVING MONEY IN CON-
NECTION WITH NAVAL RADIO SERVICE ("Radio Bond"). 1917-19. Folded
papers in bundles. 6 ft. 3 in. Unarranged.   99
    NJA 110.

RECORDS RELATING TO THE COMMANDEERING AND RELEASE OF PRIVATE VESSELS
FOR USE BY THE NAVY. 1917-19. Folded papers. 27 ft. Arranged alphabetically by names of vessels. Index to identifica-
tion numbers of vessels in front of first box.   100
    Instructions to commandants of naval districts to start negotiations
for purchase of privately owned vessels; reports and correspondence of
boards of appraisal for merchant and private vessels; certificates of
ownership; bills of sale; and other data concerning the acquisition of
private vessels and the disposition of the vessels when no longer required by the Navy.

RECORDS RELATING TO TERMINATED LEASES OF NAVAL REAL ESTATE. 1917-32.
Folders. 9 ft. Arranged numerically, 1-4330 (with many numbers
lacking). Indexed in Entry 102.   101
    Copies of leases, licenses, permits, renewals, cancellations, and
releases; requests for authority to lease and to renew leases; instruments

of purchase of leased property, with deeds and titles; and related correspondence. The numbers of the cases seem unrelated to the dates of the leases or releases. Many folders lack essential documents, such as copies of the lease.

INDEX TO LEASE FILES. 1917-32. Cards 6 x 4 in. 1 ft. 8 in. Arranged
      alphabetically by names of States in which leased property was
         situated, Alabama - North Dakota.   102
   Gives State and locality in which property is situated, lease-file number, premises of agreement, parties to agreement, terms of agreement, and notes on renewal of agreement, dates of filing of papers, and file numbers of related correspondence. The index for O-W is not found.

CLOSED NOd CONTRACTS AND BONDS (copies), WITH RELATED CORRESPONDENCE.
      1924-43. Folders. 3 ft. 9 in. Arranged by contract number.   103
   All but approximately 2 linear inches of these records concern closed contracts numbered from NOd 457 through NOd 860 (Aug. 1933 - Oct. 1936), with related correspondence as late as Apr. 1943 concerning execution of and releases from the contracts. NOd 1175 (June 1939) and a few contracts signed before 1933 are also included.

CORRESPONDENCE RELATING TO CLAIMS OF PERSONAL INJURY AND LOSS REFERRED
      TO THE JUDGE ADVOCATE GENERAL FOR HIS OPINION. 1926-34. Folders.
      1 ft. 8 in. Arranged alphabetically by claimants' names.   104
   Claims of personal injuries, loss of clothing, damage to household effects, etc., originating, in some cases, as early as the Civil War.

DATA RELATING TO UNUSED REAL-ESTATE HOLDINGS OF THE NAVY DEPARTMENT.
      1932. 2 looseleaf binders. 3 in.   105
   The first binder, "Lands Acquired by Navy Department," consists of (a) "List of Unused Properties under Control of Navy Department, April 5, 1932," giving location of each property, designation (reservation, air station, etc.), area in acres or square feet, and number of buildings (if any), arranged alphabetically by city or site, and (b) "Title Data," composed of one summary for each State, Territory, or insular possession (in a single alphabet), listing each property of the Navy therein, date when acquired, how acquired, acreage, and dates and contents of instruments by which acquired. The second binder, "Lands Disposed of by Navy Department," Apr. 25, 1932, consists apparently of matter omitted by oversight from the first.

LETTERS SENT RELATING TO NAVAL REAL ESTATE ("General Correspondence").
      Jan-Dec. 1934, Jan. 1936 - Dec. 1937. 3 stapled vols. in 3
         envelopes. 11 in. Carbon copies. Arranged chronologically.   106
   A volume for 1935 is not found. One of the envelopes is labeled "Spindle File."

D. Records Relating to Patents, 1907-1942

   Before 1917 the Navy Department was occasionally involved in litigation connected with patents, but apparently no separate bodies of records relative to patents were formed. World War I resulted in the submission of great numbers of inventions to the Navy Department. Correspondence relative to inventions was handled at first by the Naval Consulting Board, but in 1918 it was transferred to the Office of the Secretary of the Navy, where it was referred to an officer addressed as "Secretary of the Navy (Inventions)." Questions of patents and related legal matters were under the cognizance of the Office of the Solicitor of the Navy until 1921, when they were returned to the Office of the Judge Advocate General.

An act of July 1, 1918, authorized the Secretary of the Navy to pay cash rewards to civil employees for beneficial suggestions on condition that the employees execute agreements that the use of such suggestions should not form the basis of any claims against the United States by the employees or their heirs or assigns. In General Order 547, August 31, 1920, the Secretary of the Navy proclaimed that "the Government has the right to manufacture or have manufactured and use all inventions of officers and men in the Navy made while in Government service and whether patented or not," and that the Navy Department would not request Congress to provide funds for cash rewards to officers and enlisted men, though inventors and patentees in the Navy and the Navy Department retained all commercial rights to profit from their inventions and patents. This order was reprinted as General Order 35, January 5, 1921.

The effect of the order was to encourage concealment of inventions and devices. On October 4, 1929, General Order 35 was canceled by General Order 195, which referred to conditions under which the Navy Department did not have "the title to or right to use the invention" and under which its use by the Department was "proper matter for an agreement conformable to law between the Navy Department and the employee." The order continued as follows:

> In the interest of the Government every person in the naval service and every employee of the Naval Establishment who makes an invention is hereby urged to furnish information thereof to the Navy Department promptly through official channels. To assist the Navy Department in determining the rights of the Government and the inventor, a summary of the circumstances should be included in the indorsement of the commanding officer. Such information should be furnished irrespective of the rights of the individual. In cases where the Government has the title to or right to use the invention, the Navy Department will proceed with the application for letters patent in the name of the inventor to protect the interests of the Government. In cases where the Government has no title or right to use the invention, but the invention is deemed useful to the Government, the Navy Department will, on request of the inventor, undertake the prosecution of the application for letters patent upon execution of a license, of the scope previously defined, to the Government. Under other circumstances the inventor will be left free to secure a patent in such manner as he may choose.

The records described below relate chiefly to patents and inventions of officers, enlisted men, and civil employees of the Navy and the Navy Department, and include papers describing the patents and inventions, instruments securing the rights of patentees, inventors, and the Department, and related correspondence. Some of the records concern foreign patents used by the Department. Most of the records originated in the Patents Section of the Office of the Judge Advocate General, acting in cooperation with the Department of Justice. At a date subsequent to the latest patent records of the Navy Department in the National Archives, functions relative to patents were transferred from the Office of the Judge Advocate General to the Office of the Secretary of the Navy, within which they are (at the date of writing) handled by the Patents Division of the Office of Research and Inventions.

APPLICATIONS FOR LETTERS PATENT. Dec. 1907 – Nov. 1932. Booklets.   107
    5 in. Printed. Unarranged.
    Apparently only scattered items have been brought together in this small file. The applications contain descriptions and drawings.

CORRESPONDENCE AND DATA CONCERNING INVENTIONS. July 1915 – Dec. 1934.   108
    Folders. 333 ft. Arranged alphabetically by inventors' names.
    Each folder bears the name of the inventor and the title of his invention. No index of such titles is available in the National Archives. The folders contain letters received from inventors, copies of letters sent to them, pamphlets and descriptions submitted by them, plans and drawings, a printed form labeled "Memorandum of Interview," and a printed form summarizing details of each invention. The letters received are addressed to the President, the Secretary of the Navy, Congressmen, and others, and in large part are from inventors outside the Navy and the Navy Department. More than half of the letters date from 1917 and 1918.

RECORDS RELATING TO GERMAN CLAIMS OF INFRINGEMENT OF PATENT. 1918-31.   109
    Folders. 13 ft. 6 in. Indexed in Entry 113.
    Papers resulting from the Settlement of War Claims Act, Mar. 10, 1938, which related to the payment of awards made by the Mixed Claims Commission, United States and Germany (established in pursuance of an agreement made August 10, 1922, between the United States and Germany) and by the War Claims Arbiter; to claims presented against the United States by German, Austrian, and Hungarian nationals for merchant vessels, radio stations, patents, and other property commandeered by the United States during the World War; and to the return of property held by the Alien Property Custodian. The papers consist of (1) copies of correspondence of the Corporation Management Division, Office of the Alien Property Custodian, concerning German patents, 1918-27 (3 trays); (2) copies of miscellaneous papers, including reports to the Department of Justice, replies to the War Claims Arbiter, letters to bureaus, and requests for patents (17 trays); and (3) dossiers of correspondence, with copies of claims and settlements, 1929-31, arranged in the following groups: settled claims, 1-1178 (24 trays), patent seizure settlements, from I-1 through I-2474 and from II-1 through II-406 (5 trays), dismissed cases, 120-1180 (12 trays), and unfinished cases, 63-1125 (5 trays).

PATENT CASE FILES. Apr. 1918 - Dec. 1942. Envelopes. 84 ft. Arranged
        alphabetically by patentees' names (including a separate alphabet
    •   of confidential dossiers.)   110
    The printed cover of each envelope (NJA 230 and NEng 178) contains
blanks for the following information: serial number of patent, when
filed, inventor's name and address, title of invention, attorney of record, file number, date when allowed, date when patented, and list of
actions taken with date of each. On most envelopes some of the blanks
are left vacant. The envelopes contain plans and drawings, descriptions,
copies of reports of examiners to the Commissioner of Patents, notice of
allowance of claims, notices of transmittal of letters patent, amendments
to applications, and sometimes the applications themselves. No index is
available in the National Archives.

RECORDS RELATING TO INTERFERENCES ("References"). 1925-42, with papers
        as early as 1893. Envelopes and packages. 12 ft. 6 in.   111
    The papers were received by the National Archives in 60 labeled pack-
ages, the numbers and labels of which have been retained in the labeling
of the boxes. The packages bore such labels as "Norton vs. Miller vs.
Manson," "Eaton," "Airplane Running Lights," and "Mr. Naegle's Morgue"
(alphabetical, H-S), some designating particular cases and others designating inventions or classes of inventions that were matter of interference
proceedings. Some of the labels are illegible. The order of packages
seems fortuitous, unrelated to an arrangement by alphabet, chronology, or
subject. The papers are apparently such as might be introduced in evidence
or accumulated during the preparation of cases. The assembling of the
papers probably began about 1925, and many earlier papers were inserted
into the file. No index is available in the National Archives.

REPORTS OF INTERFERENCES. May 1926 - Jan. 1941. Envelopes. 4 ft. 2 in.
        Arranged by interference number, 53964-78418.   112
    Copies of papers of the Examiner of Interferences and the Board of
Appeals, United States Patent Office; correspondence of the Navy Department with the Department of Justice (including originals with file numbers
belonging to the general file of the Office of the Secretary of the Navy);
correspondence with patent attorneys; correspondence with bureaus and offices of the Navy Department; and copies of powers of attorney granted by
naval personnel to the Officer in Charge, Patent Section, Office of the
Judge Advocate General. The envelopes are printed forms with blanks for
various information, but ordinarily little is given beyond names of plaintiff and defendant, navy case number, and interference number. The navy
case numbers, as low as 157 and as high as 2304, are unrelated to the interference numbers. The records are secret and confidential. No index is
available in the National Archives.

INDEX TO GERMAN PATENT CLAIMS. 1929-31. Cards 5 x 3 in. 6 ft. 6 in.
        Variously arranged (by claimants' names, by docket number, by
        patent number, and by file number of reports to the Department of
        Justice). Index to records in Entry 109.   113

E. Records Relating to Opinions and Decisions, 1856-1911

It was a duty of the Judge Advocate General to render formal opinions upon matters of law and naval regulations submitted to him by the Secretary of the Navy, and to keep records of opinions and decisions. Few documents conveying opinions and decisions are known to have been filed in separate series; most form parts of series that are more general in subject or form.

LETTERS FROM ATTORNEYS GENERAL ("Opinions of Attorneys General"). Mar. 1856 - June 1903. 4 vols. 1 ft. Arranged chronologically. Vol. 1 indexed.   114
   Replies to questions submitted by the Secretary of the Navy.

OPINIONS ISSUED BY THE JUDGE ADVOCATE GENERAL ("Record, No. 1"). Aug. 1878 - Apr. 1884. 1 vol. 2 in. Handwritten copies. Arranged chronologically. Indexed.   115

INDEX TO DECISIONS ISSUED BY THE SECRETARY OF THE NAVY AND THE JUDGE ADVOCATE GENERAL ("Index to Decisions from 1878"). Aug. 1878 - June 1886. 1 vol. 2 in. Arranged alphabetically, chiefly by subjects but to some extent by names.   116
   Gives subject of decision or person affected by it, rank of person, date of letter conveying decision, and where letter is filed. No abstracts of the decisions are included. The letters are copied in "J. A. Record" (Entry 115), "Officers Book," "Congress Book," "Executive Book," "General Letter Book," "Flag Officers Book," "Bureau Letters," "Marine Corps Letters," and "Commandants." Of these all but the first were series maintained by the Office of the Secretary of the Navy and now (with the exception of "Marine Corps Letters," in Record Group 80) in the Naval Records Collection.

REGISTER OF DECISIONS OF THE JUDGE ADVOCATE GENERAL ("Key to Letters Received," labeled on front cover "Record of Decisions"). Dec. 1882 - Nov. 1886. 1 vol. 1 1/2 in. Arranged chronologically.   117
   Gives number and date of letter sent, to whom, address of correspondent, subject of letter, and disposition of inquiry.

DECISIONS OF THE COMPTROLLER OF THE TREASURY. May 1898 - Oct. 1904. Folded papers. 2 ft. 1 in. Arranged chronologically.   118
   Numbered letters segregated from the general file of the Office of the Judge Advocate General.

OPINIONS OF THE ATTORNEY GENERAL. Mar. 1904 - Feb. 1909. Loose papers. 2 in. Arranged chronologically.   119
   Fragments segregated from the general file.

PRINTED DECISIONS OF THE COMPTROLLER OF THE TREASURY. June 1907 - May 1910. Folded papers in 2 trays. 1 ft. 3 in. Arranged chronologically.   120
   Assembled primarily as a register, formed by detailed penciled titles and summaries in lieu of endorsements.

OPINIONS OF THE SOLICITOR OF THE NAVY ("Opinions"). June 1910 - Dec. 1911. 1 vol. 1 in. Press copies. Arranged chronologically. Indexed.   121

Chiefly memoranda to the Secretary and the Assistant Secretary of the Navy. According to a note in the front of the volume, "All previous opinions of the Solicitor are copied in the regular office books, Nos. 1 to 3 incl." (Entry 25).

F. Other Records, 1863-1929

The records listed below relate to such functions of the Judge Advocate General as were not particularly the subject of records listed in preceding subsections, or were miscellaneous rather than general.

[Miscellaneous Case File. Ca. 1863-83. 41 vols. NRC 297.]

INDEX TO MISCELLANEOUS CASE FILE ("General Index to Files, No. 1").
    Ca. 1863-83. 1 vol. 2 in. Arranged by first letter of
    subjects or of correspondents' names, thereunder in order of
    binding of the papers indexed.   122
    Gives subject or correspondent's name, rank of correspondent, subject
of communication, and where filed (volume and document number therein).
The index was evidently begun while the binding of the 41 vols. was in
progress. The bound volumes were cited in the style "A, vol. 3, no. 85,"
with some citations lacking this information and preceded by the penciled
notation "Not bound yet." Comparison of the index and the volumes shows
that when the index was compiled all of A and B was already bound and that
vol. 4 of C was bound later. The other unbound documents were not included
in the series of bound files. At the time these unbound documents were
stored in cases, boxes, and packages, occasionally referred to in penciled
notes. Their present whereabouts is unknown. The index includes no dates.

REGISTER OF CONGRESSIONAL BILLS AFFECTING THE NAVY DEPARTMENT (later
    volumes labeled "Legislation"). Feb. 1892 - Jan. 1899, Mar.
    1907 - May 1909, Mar. 1913 - June 1934. 25 vols. 2 ft. 5 in.
    Arranged by Congresses, thereunder usually by sessions.   123
    The later volumes are each in five parts: (a) and (b), House Bills
and Senate Bills, each entered alphabetically by first letter of subject,
thereunder chronologically, giving number of bill, subject, by whom and
when introduced, committee to which referred, when reported, when passed
or otherwise acted on, when introduced in the other house, when and to
what committee referred there, when reported, when passed or otherwise
acted on there, when approved, and remarks (chiefly on publication); (c)
legislation referred to the Department for comment and recommendation,
giving bill number, subject, file number of letter of transmittal, from
what committee received, when received, where referred (bureau or office),
when referred, when received back, date of mailing of reply, and character
of reply; (d) legislation originating in the Navy Department, giving bill
number, subject, file number of letter sent, when sent and when acknowledged
in each house, and remarks; and (e) legislation referred to the Bureau of
the Budget, giving bill number, subject, file number, when referred, when
received back, character of reply, when sent to Congress, and remarks. The
earlier volumes contain only a part of this information, and the first two
are cryptical and nearly illegible.

DEPARTMENTAL AND GENERAL ORDERS RECEIVED AND ISSUED. Feb. 1894 – June
    1910. 2 vols. 3 in. Arranged chronologically.   124
   Chiefly printed.

CONGRESSIONAL BILLS AND ATTACHED CORRESPONDENCE ("Congressional Corre-
    spondence"). Jan. 1900 – Dec. 1905. Folded papers. 1 ft. 3 in.
    Arranged chronologically.   125
   Numbered letters segregated from the general file.

MISCELLANEOUS PAPERS. Ca. 1901 – ca. 1925, with papers as early as
    1890. Folders and loose papers. 3 ft. 4 in. Unarranged.   126
   Chiefly loose papers and single sheets of unassembled letters, from
files of the Judge Advocate General, the Solicitor of the Navy, the Secretary of the Navy, the Chief of Naval Operations, and the Division of
Officers and Fleet of the Bureau of Navigation. Most of the letters are
stamped but not numbered. They relate somewhat more to matters under
the cognizance of the Judge Advocate General and the Solicitor of the
Navy than to other matters, but no central subject is discernible. Even
a tentative arrangement of the papers would require separate examination
of nearly every sheet.

ORDERS FOR STATIONERY AND MISCELLANEOUS SUPPLIES ("Letters," labeled on
    front cover "Stationery Letters"). July 1903 – Dec. 1911. 1 vol.
    1 1/4 in. Press copies. Arranged chronologically.   127
   Requisitions for such materials as paper, ink, typewriters, and soap,
and for such services as carpentry.

REQUISITIONS FOR PRINTING AND BINDING. Oct. 1903 – Dec. 1911. 2 vols.
    2 in. Press copies. Arranged chronologically.   128
   Includes description of the matter to be printed or bound.

III. RECORDS OF BOARDS AND OTHER SPECIAL UNITS CONCERNED WITH MATTERS UNDER THE COGNIZANCE OF THE JUDGE ADVOCATE GENERAL, 1896-1933

    The records described below were created by boards, courts, and other
special or temporary units concerned with matters of law and naval regulations and therefore under the cognizance of the Judge Advocate General or
(for matters other than personnel, 1908–21) of the Solicitor of the Navy.
These records were filed as separate series created by single units and
not combined to form series composed of records from two or more units.
The records of most courts and boards were filed by the Office of the Judge
Advocate General in large numerical series distinguished by type of court
or board, such as records of proceedings of general courts martial or of
naval and marine examining boards, described in earlier entries of this
checklist. Many of the records here listed could have been numbered and
filed as parts of these larger series.

Board of Examining Professors in Mathematics

    Appointed in compliance with an act of Congress of January 20, 1881,
with Simon Newcomb, Professor of Mathematics, USN, as President, to examine
candidates for appointment as professors of mathematics in the Navy.

[Record of Proceedings. Feb.-May 1881. 1 vol. NRC 299.]

Board To Examine Into Certain Accusations Against Officers and Employees
of the Department of Steam Engineering, New York Navy Yard

Appointed December 27, 1895, with Commo. Robert L. Phythian as Senior
Member and Lt. John J. Knapp as Recorder.

RECORD OF PROCEEDINGS. Jan. 6-20, 1896. 2 vols. 4 in. See Entry 38
     for related records.   129

Board on Revision of the Navy Regulations

The precept of the Board is not found. Its President was Capt.
Samuel C. Lemly, Judge Advocate General.

RECORDS. Apr.-Aug. 1896. Loose papers. 2 1/2 in. Unarranged.   130
   Scattered letters and memoranda, chiefly drafts of alterations in the
Navy Regulations, with comments and changes submitted or appended by
various officers and officials. The records include also a mimeographed
report (Nov. 6, 1895) of a board appointed, with Lt. Comdr. E. H. C.
Leutze as Senior Member, to carry out the provisions of Articles 1677 and
1679 of the Navy Regulations, considering "the forms best adapted for
keeping the time of employees, preparing pay rolls, identifying the men
making payments, and reporting the time and amount chargeable to each job
order."

Court of Inquiry in the Case of R. A. Winfield S. Schley

Appointed July 26, 1901, with Admiral George Dewey as President and
Capt. Samuel C. Lemly, Judge Advocate General, as Judge Advocate, to inquire into the conduct of Admiral Schley during the recent war with Spain.
The inquiry was made at the request of Admiral Schley, who submitted an
official complaint against certain assertions in The History of the Navy,
by Edgar Stanton Maclay, which had been adopted as a textbook by the Naval
Academy. The official record of the case is no. 4952 in Entry 30, in which
it constitutes the five separately bound parts of vol. 738.

LETTERS SENT ("Letters"). July 22, 1901 - Jan. 21, 1902. 1 vol. 1 in.
     Press copies. Indexed.   131
   Replies to applicants for appointment as stenographer, letters requesting copies of documents, and the like.

Examining Board of Ordnance Draftsmen

EXAMINATION PAPERS OF CANDIDATES FOR APPOINTMENT AS FIRST-CLASS ASSISTANT
     ORDNANCE DRAFTSMEN, EXAMINED DECEMBER 21, 1904, WITH ATTACHED COR-
     RESPONDENCE. Stapled folder. 6 in. Unarranged.   132
   The examination was held at the Washington Navy Yard.

Naval Disciplinary Barracks, Port Royal, S. C.

Established by orders issued August 10, 1911, with a view to improving the system of naval prison administration. Began operation September 1, 1911.

RECORDS. 1911-15. Chiefly loose papers. 6 ft. <u>133</u>
General correspondence, Oct. 1911 - Mar. 1914 (10 trays); copies of general court-martial sentences, 1912-14 (6 trays); copies of weekly reports of detentioners and probationers, 1911-15 (3 trays); copies of enlisted men's service records, 1911-14 (2 trays); and miscellaneous papers, including statements of accounts, charges for Government property, copies of summary court-martial proceedings, single-transfer accounts, reports of deposits, reports of details, copies of proceedings of deck courts, receipts for transfer papers, pay-roll vouchers, reports of the Marine command, and papers relating to furloughs, punishments, drills and instructions, indebtedness, and dispositions.

Naval Disciplinary Barracks, Puget Sound, Wash.

Established by orders issued May 9, 1912, in completion of the plan contemplated in the establishment of the Disciplinary Barracks at Port Royal.

RECORDS. 1912-15. Envelopes and flat and folded papers. 2 ft. 6 in. <u>134</u>
General correspondence, and papers relating to property, clothing, affidavits and depositions, athletics and entertainments, medals and badges, courts and boards, sentences, detentioners, transfers, ratings, and enlistments.

Board on Valuation of Commandeered Property

Appointed September 26, 1918, with E. R. Preston, Charlotte, N. C., as Chairman (succeeded March 22, 1920, by Maj. Charles R. Pollard, Delphi, Ind.), to visit such places as might be designated and to consider what compensation should be received by claimants to property and rights therein taken over for naval purposes. The Board was instructed to receive and examine the evidence submitted by claimants (both orally and in writing), to obtain full and satisfactory abstracts of title, to arrange settlement of claims whenever possible, and to report on each locality to the Solicitor of the Navy. By an order of December 1, 1921, the Board was transferred to the supervision of the Judge Advocate General. In February 1922 the Board was about to be dissolved, but no order of dissolution is found.

RECORDS. 1918-22. Volumes, looseleaf binders, folders, envelopes, and
loose papers. 49 ft. <u>135</u>
The following are arranged alphabetically by place: Arnold Farm, King George Co., Va., report, June 28, 1920; Blackstone Island, Md., hearings, Apr. 21, 1920 (1 binder), and exhibits (1 envelope); Cape May, N. J., hearings, July 1 - Aug. 28 and Oct. 7, 1920 (6 binders); Fort Mifflin, Pa., report, May 10, 1921 (1 binder); Gould Island, R. I., report (1 binder);

Great Lakes, Ill., hearings, June 15 - July 12, 1919 (4 binders), and
photographs (2 binders); Hampton Roads (Naval Operating Base), report
(1 binder); Indian Head, Md. (White Plain and Indian Head Railroad),
hearings, Apr. 7-12, 1920 (3 vols.), and report (1 binder); Parris
Island, S. C., hearings, Apr. 15-24, 1919 (2 binders), photographs (2
binders), and report (1 binder); Philadelphia, hearings (binders 1 and
3); Puget Sound, hearings, July 28 - Aug. 11, 1919 (3 binders), and
photographs (1 binder); Quantico, Va., hearings, Dec. 13, 1918 - Feb. 1,
1919 (2 binders), and report (1 binder); and Yorktown and Williamsburg,
Va. (Navy Mine Depot), hearings, Oct. 21, 1919 - Jan. 10, 1920 (5 vols.),
and report (1 binder). Bound abstracts of title, unarranged, occupy 2½
shelves. The records in the 82 boxes, which are not labeled, appear to
be grouped to some extent by place. They consist of correspondence with
individual claimants, often arranged in alphabets by claimants' names; and
appraisals, individual valuation sheets for buildings, tabulation sheets,
maps, blueprints, and exhibits submitted by claimants. A large volume
(22 x 17 x 3 in.) contains tabulations showing name of claimant, docket
number of claim, description of property in question, area, whether im-
proved or not, value of land, value of buildings, compensation asked by
owner, and valuation of property, with handwritten corrections. The card
indexes relate chiefly to claimants in particular localities. Folders
of miscellaneous matter are enclosed in a large package labeled "Appraisals,
Office Memos, etc., re Great Lakes, Lake Denmark, Cape May, Hampton Roads,
Parris Island, Yorktown." No evidence is found to indicate what may have
been the original order of any of these records.

Legal Section, Force Commander's Office, United States Naval Forces Operating in European Waters

Established August 28, 1918, by Office Memorandum 89 of the Chief of
Staff, United States Naval Forces Operating in European Waters, with Comdr.
W. H. McGrann in charge and Lt. Comdr. R. K. Wright as assistant in charge,
to handle "all matters involving Admiralty or other civil law, including
claims for damages against the United States consequent on the presence and
operation of United States Naval Forces in European countries and European
Waters." After the establishment of the London and Paris Naval Boards on
Claims (by orders dated February 12, 1919), it was a duty of the Legal Section to prepare cases for the consideration of the London Board. Though
in general the activities of the United States Naval Forces Operating in
European Waters were under the cognizance of the Chief of Naval Operations,
the presence of various papers of the Office of the Solicitor of the Navy
and later of the Office of the Judge Advocate General, intermingled with
records of the Legal Section, indicates that these records were received
and augmented by the Office of the Judge Advocate General and thus were separated from the records of the Office of the Chief of Naval Operations,
which presumably included all other records of the United States Naval
Forces Operating in European Waters. The date of dissolution of the Legal
Section is not found in the records. As received by the National Archives,
the records of the Legal Section were in complete disorder and were mixed
with alien fiscal and personnel records. They have been roughly segregated
and the more easily identifiable folders and stapled volumes have been assembled in series; but a considerable part of the records consists of single

sheets and unidentified fragments, stapled volumes that have lost outer leaves, and folders of brittle material from which the edges bearing labels have crumbled away. It therefore appears inadvisable to distinguish formally among series of which the nature and quantity cannot be precisely ascertained at present.

RECORDS. 1917-22. Folders, stapled volumes, and loose papers. 5 ft. 11 in.   136

The records may be tentatively described in the following groups: (1) Correspondence under subject numbers from 2 through 56, Sept. 1918 - Apr. 1921 (20 in.). The subjects are listed in Appendix C. (2) Cases involving collisions of United States vessels, arranged alphabetically by name of plaintiff vessel, Dec. 1917 - May 1922 (15 in.). These papers consist of reports from investigating officers, evidence submitted by claimants or collected by the Legal Section, and records of action by the Legal Section. (3) Cases received from the Legal Aide in Paris, un-arranged (5 in.). (4) A binder listing dockets of all maritime cases sent by the Legal Section to the Arbitration Board and the London and Paris Naval Boards on Claims previously to Dec. 1921, arranged alphabeti-cally by names of United States vessels and cross-indexed by names of other vessels, giving date and place of collision and action taken by the Legal Section. (5) Register of letters received, Sept. 12, 1918 - Jan. 18, 1919 (1 stapled vol. and loose papers). (6) "Log, Legal Section," and chronological copies of letters sent, Jan. 1919 - Dec. 1921, inter-mingled with reports of activities of the Legal Section and with torn and crumpled loose papers and fragments. It seems probable that other records of the Legal Section may have been overlooked when those here listed were recovered from masses of unlabeled and in part unidentified matter.

Paris Naval Board on Claims

Appointed by a letter of the Assistant Secretary of the Navy, February 12, 1919, with Capt. T. T. Craven (succeeded by Capt. George C. Shafer and R. A. T. P. Magruder) as Senior Member, "to consider, adjust and dispose of matters involving financial liability of the United States arising from activities during the War and demobilization of United States Naval Forces in European Waters and on land." The duties of the Board included "settle-ments of property losses or damages incidental to occupation of buildings and lands," "financial matters relative to the demobilization of Naval material in France" (sale or other disposal), "the concluding of all con-tractual obligations arising from demobilization," and "the adjustment of claims for damage to persons and private property occasioned and caused by Naval personnel." Commanding officers of bases, detachments, or stations in which obligations arose or had arisen were to cause investigations to be made, collect facts, prepare necessary documents, and submit complete reports, with their recommendations regarding liability and the amount there-of, to the Legal Aide, Staff Representative's Office, Paris, by whom the papers were to be transmitted, with recommendations, to the Board. The Board was "directly under the Assistant Secretary of the Navy," but its papers were evidently received and augmented by the Office of the Solicitor. By order of the Secretary of the Navy, April 16, 1920, the power of the

Board was vested in R. A. T. P. Magruder, Naval Attaché, Paris; and the Board was formally dissolved at its meeting of June 15, 1920. It appears to have continued to meet informally, for an order of the Secretary directed to the Staff Representative, United States Naval Forces Operating in European Waters, Forces in France, June 4, 1921, directed that the Board be dissolved as of July 1, 1921. Its records were forwarded to the Secretary of the Navy June 28, 1921. Unfinished business was left in the hands of the Naval Attaché, Paris.

MINUTES. Feb. 25, 1919 – June 15, 1920, with reports till Dec. 1, 1920.
    2 folders. 2 1/2 in. Arranged chronologically.   **137**
    Minutes of meetings 1-64 (Feb. 25, 1919 – June 15, 1920) and reports of Rear Admiral Magruder, July 31 – Dec. 1, 1920. The minutes consist chiefly of reports of action on each claim considered at each meeting.

RECORDS OF CLAIMS CASES. 1918-22. Folders. 6 ft. 10 in. Arranged by
    case number, 1-432.   **138**
    Statements and evidence submitted by claimants; translations; copies of leases, deeds, and other legal instruments; excerpts from minutes of the Board indicating action on each claim; record of payment of claim; and correspondence. No index to the claim is found, though those that were acted on are summarized in the minutes.

MISCELLANEOUS RECORDS. 1919-21. 3 folders. 2 1/2 in.   **139**
    A few letters concerning the history of the Board; list of claims not acted on; and data concerning the collision of the SS Norwege and the USS Western Comet.

London Naval Board on Claims

    Appointed by a letter of the Assistant Secretary of the Navy, February 12, 1919, with Capt. E. C. Tobey, Pay Corps, as Senior Member, and with instructions nearly identical with those of the Paris Naval Board on Claims, appointed on the same date. The Board received reports from commanding officers through the Legal Section, Force Commander's Office, United States Naval Forces Operating in European Waters. It was concerned with Great Britain and with European countries other than France, and after June 1920 it also received cases from France. It was dissolved as of July 1, 1921.

MINUTES ("Official Record of Proceedings"). Feb. 26, 1919 – June 29, 1921.
    1 stapled vol. and loose papers. 1 in.   **140**
    Chiefly summaries of action taken on each case at each meeting.

REGISTERS OF LETTERS RECEIVED. Dec. 1918 – Dec. 1919. 1 folder and 1
    stapled vol. 2 in. Arranged chronologically.   **141**
    Within the period included by both the stapled volume (Dec. 1918 – Dec. 1919) and the folder (Feb. 1 – Nov. 26, 1919), approximately the same matter seems to be registered, but the two records appear independent of each other. The former may have been maintained by the Legal Section, and later turned over to the Board. The folder is labeled "Chronological"; the volume is unlabeled, and may have lost outer leaves. Each gives date when claims papers were received, from whom, abstract, and action taken.

COPIES OF CERTAIN CORRESPONDENCE. Feb. 1919 - May 1920. 2 folders and
    1 stapled vol. 2 1/2 in.   142
    Copies of outgoing and of incoming cablegrams, Mar. 1919 - May 1920
(1 folder each), and of letters sent, Apr. 1 - May 31, 1919.

FILE OF CLAIMS ORIGINATING AT SEA. 1919-21. Folders. 6 ft. Arranged
    by first letter of names of U. S. ships.   143
    Chiefly papers submitted to the Board by claimants asking damages for
losses caused by United States ships, through collision or otherwise.
Some of the cases are numbered, others not.

FILE OF CLAIMS ORIGINATING ON LAND. 1919-21. Loose papers and stapled
    volumes. 2 ft. 11 in. Arranged alphabetically by claimants'
    names.   144
    Matter forwarded by commanding officers to the Legal Section and thence,
with recommendations and notes, to the Board, occasionally with a record
of action taken by the Board. Guide sheets, bearing the letters of the
alphabet, are labeled "Land Cases." Case numbers are appended to the records.

REGISTER OF CLAIMS. Feb. 28, 1919 - Apr. 25, 1921. 4 stapled vols.
    (ribbon copy and 3 duplicates). 1 in. Arranged numerically, 1-
    421.   145
    Gives claimant's name, number of claim, character of claim, action taken
by Board, settlement made, amount claimed, and amount awarded.

INDEX TO CLAIMS. Feb. 1919 - Apr. 1921. 1 folder. 1/4 in. Arranged
    alphabetically by claimants' names.   146
    Gives names of parties to claim, claim number, nature of claim, amount,
and disposition.

REGISTER OF ACTION TAKEN ON CLAIMS. 1919-21. 1 folder. 1 1/2 in.   147
    One sheet for each claim, giving claim number, claimant's name, place
and date of alleged injury, nature of injury, party at fault, amount claimed,
and settlement made. The sheets are arranged in three classes (A, B, and
C), the signification of which is not designated; under these they appear
to be unarranged.

MISCELLANEOUS RECORDS. 1919-22. Folders, stapled volumes, and loose
    papers. 2 ft.   148
    SS Brinkburn vs. USS Great Northern, 1918-21; claims arising from
cancellation of contracts entered into by the U. S. Navy with firms in
Great Britain; force instructions, Bureau of Navigation circular letters,
office memoranda, etc.; Lieutenant Foster, extra papers from; French
Arbitration Board, Apr.-May 1921; French situation, general; SS Kurland
vs. USS George Henry, Dec. 1918 - May 1922; memoranda on cancellation of
contract claims; miscellaneous admiralty contracts; miscellaneous cases
referred to Board; miscellaneous memoranda; miscellaneous opinions on
matters of contract and salvage; Operations, vessels damaged in action,
Cassin; preliminary cables and miscellaneous memoranda about Board; SS
Rosedale vs. USS Luella, Apr.-June 1919; SS War Weapon vs. USS Lake Clear,
1918-22; various claims numbered from 1 through 407, including only a few
numbers, some of which could be added to the sea or land claims file; and
unlabeled loose materials.

Board on Submarine Claims

Established May 13, 1920, with Capt. William J. Baxter, Chief Constructor, as Senior Member, to examine and report upon claims of the Electric Boat Co., Groton, Conn., under contracts for submarines. The main report of the Board was dated Feb. 17, 1921.

RECORDS. May 1920 – Nov. 1922. 1 folder, 2 envelopes, and loose papers. 4 in. Unarranged.   149
   Fragments of copies of the report, with correspondence, exhibits, and printed or photostated copies of contracts, Feb. 8, 1917 – Nov. 21, 1922. Some of this matter was apparently added to the file after the dissolution of the board.

Interdepartmental Radio Board

Appointed by the Secretary of War, the Secretary of the Navy, and the Attorney General, February 12, 1921, with Comdr. Stanford C. Hooper and Lt. Comdr. Edward H. Loftin as Naval members, "to investigate, hear and examine the questions relating to the liability involved in the use by the Government of patents on radio apparatus and similar devices and render to the several heads of the departments mentioned their conclusions and recommendations therein."

RECORDS. 1921–22, with a few papers as early as 1915. Folders, envelopes, and looseleaf binders. 2 ft. 1 in. Unarranged.   150
   Correspondence and memoranda of the Board, 1921-22 (folders); papers relating to patents and patent applications of Leonard F. Fuller and others for inventions relating to wireless telegraphy, 1915-18 (envelopes); and lists of patents with printed applications, one binder for each of the following: radio patents relating to underground and underwater antenna systems, compiled by Radio Research and Patent Section, Radio Division, Bureau of Steam Engineering; patents of Lee De Forest; patents relating to arc radio systems; patents relating to valves, tubes, and bulbs; antenna systems, excluding underground systems; distant control of objects by radio; heterodyne; radio patents purchased from Alien Property Custodian; assignment of Seibt Patent 1,216,615 and Reuthe Patent 1,214,591; sale of Sayville Radio Station and Atlantic Communication Co. patents to the United States; confirmations of Atlantic Communication Co. title to patents transferred to Navy formerly assigned to Gesellschaft für Drahtlose Telegraphie; patents purchased by Navy from Atlantic Communication Co. (2 binders); Vreeland Patent 1,239,852 and application no. 58,100; New York Patents Exploitation Corp.; Dr. Louis Cohen; Liberty Electric Corp.; J. Harris Rogers and H. H. Lyon; and F. A. Kolster Radio Direction Finder.

Board To Consider Claims of the Electric Boat Company
Under Contracts for Submarines

The Board, with R. A. D. W. Taylor, Chief Constructor, as Senior Member, was instructed June 21, 1922, to examine the claims of the Electric Boat Co., Groton, Conn., already reported upon by the Board on Submarine Claims.

REPORTS. Sept. 13, 1922. 2 stapled vols. 1 in. Typed copies.   151
    Two reports of the same date.

East Camp Claims Board

    Appointed June 19, 1923, with R. A. Harry H. Rousseau as Senior Member,
as "Board To Consider and Determine Questions Relating to the Just Compensation for Use and Occupancy by the United States for Naval Purposes of
Property Within East Camp, Hampton Roads, Virginia."

RECORDS. Aug.-Sept. 1923, with a few records as early as July 1921 and
        as late as Sept. 1925. Bound volumes and bundles. 2 ft. 9 in.
                                                                           152
        Unarranged.
    Transcript of testimony before the Board, Aug. 1-10, 1923 (2 copies);
report of the Board via the Bureau of Yards and Docks and the Judge Advocate General to the Secretary of the Navy, Sept. 29, 1923 (carbon copy);
bound blueprint exhibits; blueprints, maps, and printed reports of the
Board (1 bundle); cards and jackets relating to claimants (1 bundle);
"Station Correspondence" (1 bundle); and "General Correspondence, Reports
of Board, Newspaper Clippings, Memoranda, etc." (1 bundle). The last contains folders in alphabetical order, with such subjects as awards, bills,
"general correspondence," newspaper clippings, and telegrams, some of the
materials belonging to the Board and others apparently added by the Office
of the Judge Advocate General after the Board was dissolved.

Cancellation Board

    Appointed July 20, 1923, with R. A. Washington L. Capps, Chief Con-
structor, as Senior Member, to examine claims originating in the cancellation of Naval contracts. All members of the Board were also members of the
Compensation Board, and the records were filed under numbers belonging to
the general file of that Board but were maintained as a physically separate
file. The name of the Cancellation Board is not found in the records after
August 30, 1924. The Compensation Board itself was a more or less permanent
unit within the Office of the Secretary of the Navy, independent of the Office of the Judge Advocate General; its records are in Record Group 80, General Records of the Department of the Navy.

RECORDS. 1923-24, with a few records as early as Jan. 1917 and as late
        as Jan. 1931. Folders and folded papers. 2 ft. 11 in. Arranged
        numerically from 409-3(A) through Y-409-3(A), with unnumbered
        materials at the end.   153
    The numbered papers, labeled "Scrapped Vessels--Cancellation Claims,"
consist of folders for the Fore River Shipbuilding Corp., the General
Electric Co., the Newport News Shipbuilding and Dry Dock Co., the Westing-
house Electric and Mfg. Co., and the New York Shipbuilding Corp., with
statements of claims, supporting papers, and data concerning settlement of
the claims.

Naval War Claims Board

Established by order of the Secretary of the Navy April 24, 1925, with R. A. Washington L. Capps, Chief Constructor, as Senior Member, to consider claims of contractors for losses in connection with Naval contracts during the World War, as provided in an act of March 4, 1925. Three members of the Board were members of the Compensation Board.

GENERAL FILE. Apr. 1925 - Apr. 1938. Folders. 1 ft. 8 in. Arranged, by Navy Filing Manual, from (QB)L4-3/1-1 to (QB)L4-3/17.   154
  Correspondence, reports, minutes, rules of procedure, and matter filed under the names of the several members of the Board.

LETTERS SENT. May 1925 - July 1933. Stapled volumes. 10 in. Carbon copies. Arranged chronologically.   155
   (1) "Day File," May 4, 1925 - July 25, 1933 (6 stapled vols.), and (2) "Tickler File," May 20, 1925 - July 25, 1933 (5 stapled vols.). Each file contains a few letters not found in the other.

NUMERICAL CLAIMS FILE. May 1925 - Apr. 1938. Folders. 10 ft. Arranged serially by claim number from (QB)L4-3(1)-(4) to (QB)L4-3(78), thereunder chronologically.   156
  Documents, reports, blueprints, and correspondence. The first claim was received by the Board May 5, 1925; the last, June 20, 1928. Some of the claims were still under consideration several years later.

REGISTER OF CLAIMS AND OF RELATED CORRESPONDENCE. May 1925 - Mar. 1933. 3 looseleaf binders. 5 in. Arranged by claim number from 1 to 78, thereunder chronologically.   157

DRAFTS AND SUPPLEMENTARY PAPERS RELATING TO CLAIMS. May 1925 - May 1929. Folders. 5 ft. 10 in.   158
   (1) "Additional and Duplicate Papers," arranged alphabetically by claimants, June 1925 - May 1929 (7 boxes); (2) working papers, arranged alphabetically by claimants, 1925-29, chiefly penciled and undated (4 boxes); (3) copies of claimants' petitions, arranged alphabetically by claimants, May 1925 - June 1928 (1 box); (4) copies of bills of particulars with covering letters from claimants, arranged by claim number from 8 to 77, May 1925 - June 1928 (1 box); (5) rough drafts of letters, arranged chronologically, May 1925 - Apr. 1929 (1 folder); and (6) rough drafts of the Board's briefs, arranged alphabetically by claimants, May 1925 - Apr. 1929 (5 folders).

ALPHABETICAL CLAIMS FILE. Feb. 1927 - Feb. 1935 (with copies of documents of earlier date). Folders. 5 ft. 5 in. Arranged alphabetically by claimants' names.   159
  Reports from the Board to the Secretary of the Navy or the Judge Advocate General, with a copy of each "reference" referred to in each report.

MISCELLANEOUS RECORDS. 1925-29. Folders. 5 in.   160
  Precept establishing the Naval War Claims Board, Apr. 24, 1925; Public Bill No. 611, 68th Congress; extra copies of minutes; rules of procedure for investigating claims, Oct. 12, 1925; reports by the Board returned by

the Judge Advocate General; the Department's letter of Apr. 19, 1929; the Board's letter of Apr. 27, 1929; extra copies of letter on procedure, Oct. 16, 1927; references by stenographers; extra copies of the Comptroller's decision of Aug. 9, 1924; and other duplicates.

Naval Membership of the American Delegation to the International Conference on Safety of Life at Sea

An invitation from the Government of His Britannic Majesty to the Government of the United States to take part in an international conference to be held at London to consider measures for promoting the safety of life at sea was transmitted to the Department of State by the British Ambassador on September 30, 1927. A letter announcing plans for such a conference was addressed by the Secretary of State to the Secretary of the Navy on November 11, 1927. A preliminary meeting of representatives of departments and agencies concerned was held on January 12, 1928; and during the fourteen months that followed, various committees were organized to collect data and prepare recommendations. The American Delegation to the Conference consisted of the Hon. Wallace H. White, Jr., Chairman; R. A. George H. Rock, Assistant Chief of the Bureau of Construction and Repair, and Capt. Clarence S. Kempff, Hydrographer of the United States, representing the Navy Department; and representatives of various other departments and agencies. Final instructions to the Delegation were issued by the Secretary of State on March 28, 1929, addressed to the American members of "The International Conference for the Revision of the Convention of 1914 for the Safety of Life at Sea." The Conference was convened at London April 15, 1929, and adjourned May 29.

RECORDS RELATING TO THE CONFERENCE. 1927-29. Envelopes. 1 ft. 11 in. <u>161</u>
These records, almost entirely printed and processed, are not strictly records of the Conference or of the American Delegation, but may be regarded as file copies of matter accumulated by the Naval members of the Delegation and transmitted by them to the Navy Department to be filed by the Judge Advocate General, who had cognizance over the participation of the Department in international conferences. Names of members of the Delegation or of technical assistants attached to the Delegation are written in pencil on some of the pamphlets and mimeographed copies in this file. The envelopes are labeled as follows: "Miscl. Documents, Plenary Minutes, etc."; "Various American Proposals Taken to London," including reports of preliminary committees; "Copy of the Minutes of the Navigation Committee of the American Delegation Meeting at Washington," otherwise known as the Rules of the Road Committee, Oct. 30 - Dec. 4, 1928; "Meeting of the American Delegation in Washington Prior to Sailing" (pamphlets); "American Proposals on Safety of Navigation Taken to London, on Rules of the Road, Navigational Aids, Meteorology, and Ice Patrol" (2 envelopes); "Files of Subcommittee on Rules of Road and Navigational Aids"; "Minutes, Notes, and Report of Informal Conference on the Convention of Safety at Sea, 1914," copied by the U. S. Shipping Board and circulated for its members, Apr. 28, 1929 (so labeled, but actually concerned only with the Informal Conference on the Convention on Safety of Life at Sea, held at London, Nov.-Dec. 1921); "Draft 16 of Conference Report and State Dept. Print of Final Document," the latter May 31, 1929; "Complete Set of Minutes of Safety Navigation Committee," Apr. 19 - May 16, 1929 (printed); "Confidential Letter of State Dept. of Instruction Addressed to American

42

Delegates," Mar. 28, 1929 (mimeographed); "Proposals of Different Governments" (printed); and "Meeting 1 to 38 of the Am. Delegation while in London," Apr. 15 - May 29, 1929. A file maintained by Rear Admiral Rock is in the National Archives with the records of the Bureau of Construction and Repair in Record Group 19, Records of the Bureau of Ships. Correspondence relating to the Conference is filed in the general file of the Office of the Secretary of the Navy under A19/EM.

Board of Appraisal for the Appalachian Electric Power Company

Appointed in compliance with an act of May 11, 1928, with three members (one appointed by the Secretary of the Navy [Capt. William A. Merritt], one by the Company, and one by the other two members), to appraise the value of property of the Navy Department at Cabin Creek, W. Va., operated by the Appalachian Power and Electric Co. (later the Appalachian Electric Power Co.) under a contract of October 16, 1924, and renewals thereof, furnishing electric current to the Naval Ordnance Plant at South Charleston, W. Va.

RECORDS. May 1928 - Mar. 1929. Loose papers. 8 in. Unarranged. 162
Blueprints, printed briefs, fragmentary correspondence, bulky exhibits, and copies of parts of the report of the Board.

Commission for Hearing and Determining of Claims by British Nationals

Appointed by the Secretary of War July 11, 1932, with Lt. Col. Joseph I. McMullen, Judge Advocate General's Department, as Chairman, and with Lt. Comdr. Robert A. Lavender, Office of the Judge Advocate General of the Navy, as a member, to settle claims of British nationals against the United States for use of patented processes or articles during the World War. The Commission sat at London August 2-11, 1932. Apparently certain cases were prepared by a Navy Evidence Committee, the precise status of which is left uncertain by the incompleteness of the records.

PAPERS RELATING TO PATENT CLAIMS OF CITIZENS OF GREAT BRITAIN ("British War Claims File"). July 1932 - Feb. 1933. Folders and envelopes. 3 ft. 9 in. Arranged by claim number, 1-16. 163
Most of the folders and envelopes are marked with the name of Commander Lavender. Most of the records appear to be duplicates, of which the originals may have been retained by the War Department. The records include claimant's brief, brief of Crown Counsel F. Bruce McMullen, Commission's work sheet, stenographic transcript of proceedings of the Commission, claimant's evidence, transcript of testimony, Admiralty correspondence, and ex-gratia awards for claims numbered as follows: 1 (John Leopold Brodie), 2 (Lt. J. C. F. Davidson, RN), 3(Percy L. H. Davis), 4(Sir Eustace Henry Tennyson d'Eyncourt and Thomas Graham), 5 (Comdr. Alban Lewis Gwynne, RN, and Robert Alexander Sturgeon), 6 (Commander Gwynne and Herbert John Taylor), 7 (Sir James Henderson), 8 (Lt. W. D. Kilroy, RN), 9 (Lt. Col. Guy Liddell, RD), 10 (Lt. Col. Henry Newton), 11 (Robert A. Sturgeon), 12 (John I. Thornycroft & Co.), 13 (R. A. Cecil Usborne, RN), 14 (Comdr. Gerard B. Riley, RN, Comdr. Carleton C. Sherman, RN, and Lt. Comdr. Herbert O. Mock, RN), and 16 (Ernest T. Hiscock). Claim 15 is not found.

APPENDIXES

APPENDIX A

Records of the Office of the Judge Advocate General in the General File of the Office of the Secretary of the Navy (Record Group 80)

On and after April 1, 1908, the correspondence and related materials of the Office of the Judge Advocate General was consolidated with that of the Office of the Secretary of Navy in a single file, which from July 1, 1908, to September 1, 1921, included also the correspondence of the Office of the Solicitor. The original file was that of the Office of the Secretary of the Navy, begun with no. 1 on January 1, 1897. During the period before 1908 the Office of the Judge Advocate General had maintained separate general files, of which the last was discontinued on March 31, 1908. The numbers in the combined general file, as in the general file of the Secretary's Office before 1908, designated subjects rather than individual letters. Most of the subject numbers pertaining to business of the Office of the Judge Advocate General were added to the file in April 1908, beginning with no. 26250. These numbers were unrelated to those in the previous separate file of the Office of the Judge Advocate General. The numbers that are listed alphabetically by subject below contain correspondence relating chiefly to matters under the cognizance of the Judge Advocate General. The list is limited to numbers designating records that occupy not less than 2 trays (5 inches). It is not to be understood that the list contains all numbers under which correspondence of the Office of the Judge Advocate General is filed, or that all correspondence under the numbers cited is confined to that Office. The combination was continued to no. 29465, after which, in August 1926, the general file of the Secretary's Office, 1897-1926, was succeeded by that of 1926 to date. In the latter, which is under the Navy Filing Manual, the same combination has been maintained; subjects relating chiefly to the functions of the Office of the Judge Advocate General may be recognized if sought in the Manual. The part of the latter file that is later than 1940 has not been transferred to the National Archives. At a date subsequent to 1940 the Office of the Judge Advocate General discontinued the practice of filing its correspondence with that of the Office of the Secretary of the Navy.

Acquisition and demobilization of vessels 28905
Back pay 26803
Bad-conduct discharges 26838
Bills, House of Representatives 26255; Senate 26256
Bonds of disbursing officers in Naval Militia organizations 28406; of enlisted men or naval employees receiving money on account of Naval Radio Service 28567; of pay clerks, Naval Reserve Force 28958; of pay clerks, USN 28959; of pay officers 26284; of pay officers, Naval Reserve Force 28758; annual contract bonds 17271
Citizenship 26252
Claims, miscellaneous 26893
Clothing, personal property, etc., lost or destroyed 26514
Collisions, groundings, etc. 26835; collisions at sea 9204
Commandeering of vessels 28806

Contractors in default 26819

Contracts, Boston Navy Yard 26827; Charleston Navy Yard, 26547; Chelsea Naval Hospital 27239; Great Lakes Training Station 26814; Guantanamo 27450; Indian Head Proving Ground 26279; Mare Island Navy Yard 26805; Marine Corps 26275; miscellaneous 26801; Naval Academy 26833; naval coal depots 26839; Naval Ordnance Plant, Charleston, W. Va. 21931; New Fort Lyon and Las Animas Hospital 26298; New York Navy Yard 26268; Newport Training and Torpedo Station 26528; Norfolk Navy Yard 26502; Philadelphia Navy Yard 26523; Portsmouth Navy Yard 26808; Puget Sound Navy Yard 26273; Washington Navy Yard 26811; contracts for erection of wireless telegraph stations 26816; for ordnance 26548; with masters for collier personnel 27204

Courts and boards 27207; procedure 12821

Decisions of Comptroller General 26254

Deck courts 27217

Delivery of enlisted men to civil authorities 26524

Deserters, miscellaneous matter relating to 26516

Desertions, Civil War 26539

Discharge, requests for 9445

Dry Dock No. 1, Pearl Harbor 26159

Examining boards for candidates for acting ensign 28743; acting warrant officer (electricians) 28708; assistant civil engineer 28254; boatswain 28725; carpenter 28720; chaplain 27208; Dental Corps 28408; draftsman 12148; ensign 26829; Fleet Marine Corps Reserve 28737; Fleet Naval Reserve 28707; machinist 28702; Marine Corps Reserve 28781; Medical Corps 26258; Medical Reserve Corps 28426; Naval Auxiliary Reserve 28732; Naval Constructors Corps 26405; Naval Militia officers 28709; Naval Reserve 29456, 29464; ordnance gunner 28724; pay clerk 28554; Pay Corps 26544, 27223; pharmacist 28741;

quartermaster clerk, Marine Corps 28756; radio gunner 28923; second lieutenant, Marine Corps 28730

Examining boards, personnel of 26521

Frauds, graft, etc. 21355

General court-martial orders 28206

General court-martial procedure 26509

General courts martial, recommendations for 26251

Government property, reimbursement for loss of 18140

Habeas corpus proceedings 26522

Ideas, schemes, inventions, plans, etc., miscellaneous, and of no importance 26840

Judgments in Court of Claims, list of 26280

Land 8483; Newport Hospital 26636; Washington Navy Yard 19574

Laws of Navy and Marine Corps 9386

Letters in behalf of men whose cases have not been received 27228

Line of duty and misconduct status, questions concerning 29372

Naval witnesses summoned to appear in civil and naval courts 26276

Navy regulations, requests for interpretation of 26806

Officers on duty in JAG, orders for transfer, etc. 28259

Official signatures to legal papers 26802

Pardons requested 26282

Patents, infringements on 26817

Pay, checkages of 22465

Petitions and calls from Court of Claims 26266

Precepts and changes in personnel, courts of inquiry 28028; examining boards 28026; general courts martial 28025; retiring boards 28027

Prison, Cavite, 17390; Mare Island 12584; Norfolk 26546; Parris Island 28940; Portsmouth 26288; Port Royal Disciplinary Barracks and Marine Barracks 28267; Puget Sound Disciplinary Barracks 28373

Prisoners, miscellaneous matter relating to 26287

Prisoners, claims for clothing and transportation of discharged 27222

Prisons, State 26265

Prisons, prison regulations, and other prison matters 26267

Prize money, requests for 26291

Prize money and prizes 27835

Proposals, bids, etc., for naval supplies for yards and stations 28233

Records of general courts martial from stations 26262

Records of proceedings of boards of inquest 26250; of boards of investigation 26283; of examining boards for promotion of officers 26260; of retiring boards 26253

Records requested for use in civil courts 12475

Repairs to German vessels seized by the U. S. during war with Germany 28777

Report of fitness 25675

Requests for copies of papers relating to courts martial 26263; for general court-martial records 26261; for information by Auditor and Comptroller General in general and summary court-martial cases 27210

Resolutions, House and Senate 8369

Retirement, retired officers, and retired list, miscellaneous matter pertaining to 27231

Rules of the road 9398

Service and pension records, requests for and concerning 26510

Stenographers employed on general court-martial work, employment and retirement of 26271

Surety and surety companies 26257; American Surety Co. 26294; Maryland Casualty Co. 28017; National Surety Co. 26511

Taking over of vessels of Netherlands registry 28967

Vessels of nations with whom U. S. is at war, relative to taking over of by U. S. 28785

War-risk insurance 28909

APPENDIX B

Cases in "Navy Yard Cases" (Entry 29)

Vol. 1

1. Merit Jordan, Naval Storekeeper; Benjamin Spratley, Master Armorer; James A. Williams, Master Ship Joiner; John B. Davis, Master Mast- and Sparmaker; Merritt S. Moore, Master Gun-Carriage Maker; and John Hobday, Master Painter—all employed at the Gosport Navy Yard, Mar.- Aug. 1841
2. John Hobday, Master Painter, Gosport Navy Yard, Apr.-May 1852
3. Merritt S. Moore, Master Gun-Carriage Maker, Gosport Navy Yard, Oct.- Nov. 1849
4. Thomas Copeland, Steam Engineer, Gosport Navy Yard, June-July 1849

Vol. 2

5. Eben Ford, Master Blacksmith, Boston Navy Yard, Dec. 1849
6. William Merrifield, Master Blacksmith, New York Navy Yard, Feb. 1854
7. Henry Herbert, Master Bricklayer, Gosport Navy Yard, Aug. 1856
8. D. S. Grice, contractor delivering white-oak plank to the Philadelphia Navy Yard, Oct. 1861
9. Acting Volunteer Lt. W. L. Stone, making charges against officers of the USS Wamsutta, and they against him, Philadelphia Navy Yard, Mar. 1862
10. Robert W. Steele, Master Carpenter, New York Navy Yard, Dec. 1863
11. Enoch S. Davis and Charles N. Barstow, former employees of Boston Navy Yard, making charges against officials thereof, Apr. 1863
12. James W. Blaylock, Master Joiner, Philadelphia Navy Yard, Feb.-Mar. 1864
13. Thomas H. Smith, Master Boiler Maker, Washington Navy Yard, Mar. 1864

Vol. 3

14. William M. Lewis, Master Blockmaker, Boston Navy Yard, Mar. 1864
15. John Mitchell, Master Blockmaker, New York Navy Yard, Sept. 1864
16. Joseph M. Downing, Master Joiner, Washington Navy Yard, Dec. 1864
17. Timothy Murphy, Steward, Naval Hospital, Chelsea, Mass., May 1865
18. J. D. Wiggin, Master Smith, Boston Navy Yard, Dec. 1865
19. Daniel P. Pettit, Master Joiner, and others, Philadelphia Navy Yard, July 1866 and Jan. 1868
20. Joseph Willard, Foreman Blockmaker, Philadelphia Navy Yard, July 1866

Vol. 4

21. William W. Nichols, late Master Founder, Boston Navy Yard, Jan. 1867
22. Richard Van Voorhis, Sailmaker, New York Navy Yard, Apr. 1867
23. N. H. Baylis, Clerk in Storekeeper's Department, New York Navy Yard, July 1867
24. Theodore Webster, Engineer's Department, and Edward Fry, Constructor's Department, New York Navy Yard, Jan. 1868
25. Stolen tobacco and tea, Philadelphia Navy Yard, Apr. 1868

Vol. 5

26. John Roach & Sons, selling tools to Philadelphia Navy Yard, July-Aug. 1868
27. Capt. C. D. Hebb, USMC, and A. F. Clapp, Superintendent of Improvements, Pensacola Navy Yard, Aug. 1871
28. Equipment Department, Boston Navy Yard, July 1874

Vol. 6

29. George W. Cook, late Foreman of Shipwrights, Boston Navy Yard, Jan.-Feb. 1881

APPENDIX C

Subject Headings in the Subject File of the Legal Section, Force Commander's Office, United States Naval Forces Operating in European Waters, 1918-1921 (Entry 136)

Certain numbers are lacking from the file as now assembled but are presumed to have been formerly represented and are therefore entered in the list without the designation of a subject.

1
2 Aviation—lands and contracts
3
4 Base Hospital No. 3—lands and contracts
5 Base Hospital No. 4—lands and contracts
6 Bases 17 and 18, Mine Force—lands and contracts
7 Killingholme—lands and contracts
8 Eastleigh—lands and contracts
9
10 Aviation—Italy
11 Base 6, U. S. Naval Barracks, Ballybricken—agreement
12 Lands and contracts, Great Britain, general
13 Northern Bombing Group, Nos. 1-8
14 Bordeaux, France, reports from on claims for damages
15 Base 27, Plymouth—lands and contracts
16
17 Admiralty—German ships
18 Admiralty—definition of territorial waters
19 Base 29, Cardiff
20 Crews of merchant vessels
21 Memorandum of claims received, from central files
22 Claims for damages—general information
23
24 Compassionate payments
25 Demobilization, Southampton

26 Demobilization, Legal Section
27 Definition of faits de guerre
28 Courts martial
29 Legal Section, Italy
30 Joint Arbitration Board
31 Office routine
32 Reports of London Naval Board on Claims
33 London Naval Board on Claims—general
34 U. S. Naval Headquarters, London—general
35 Liquidation Commission
36 Commander McGrann, Base 29 file
37 Base Hospital No. 3, Leith
38 Mailing regulations
39 Organization of Legal Section
40 Miscellaneous opinions, Legal Section
41 Legal Section, personnel
42 Legal Section, Paris
43 Paris Naval Board on Claims
44 Legal Section, requisitions
45 Assistant Secretary Roosevelt
46 Reports on claims for damages
47 Liaison Officer, R. R. & C. tours
48 Reports of Legal Section
49 Reports on conferences at Headquarters
50 Daily reports, Legal Section
51 Salvage agreements
52
53 U. S. Shipping Board
54 Workmen's Compensation Act
55 Lieutenant Commander Wright
56 Miscellaneous unclassified

NM-55

GENERAL SERVICES ADMINISTRATION
NATIONAL ARCHIVES AND RECORDS SERVICE
THE NATIONAL ARCHIVES

Supplement to Preliminary Checklist 32

Records of the Office
of the
Judge Advocate General (Navy)

(Record Group 125)

Compiled by

Harry Schwartz

1965

INTRODUCTION

After the issuance of a preliminary checklist, it is sometimes necessary to bring the information up to date before further study can be made. Dates or quantities of records may need to be corrected, or entries for additional series may need to be inserted. This supplement to Preliminary Checklist 32 has been prepared to take care of any such changes that should be made in the original issuance and needs to be used in conjunction with it.

Corrected entries bear the original entry numbers and are in numerical order. Each entry usually contains only the title, inclusive dates, and quantity of records; the specific changes are marked by underscoring. Changes of a purely editorial nature are not being made.

Additional entries bear the original entry numbers to which suffixes A, B, C, and so on have been added to indicate the most appropriate place in the original issuance for their insertion. Center and side headings from the original issuance are repeated when needed for guidance.

In 1945, when Preliminary Checklist 32 was prepared, certain series of records created or inherited by the Office of the Judge Advocate General (Navy) had been placed in Record Group 45, Naval Records Collection of the Office of Naval Records and Library, and they were described in the checklist for that record group. For purposes of cross-references, however, they were entered in Preliminary Checklist 32 in abbreviated form. These cross-reference entries were placed in brackets and were not assigned entry numbers. In 1954 six of the series were reallocated to Record Group 125, Records of the Office of the Judge Advocate General (Navy). They are described in this supplement in entries numbered 1A through 1E and 26B. The order of listing corresponds to the one in the original issuance, where the items were entered as cross-references following entry 1 and preceding entry 27.

The volume of textual records in this record group has been increased to 2,704 cubic feet, compared with 2,696 cubic feet reported in the original issuance in 1945.

1

PRELIMINARY CHECKLIST

I. RECORDS TRANSFERRED TO THE OFFICE OF THE JUDGE ADVOCATE GENERAL

A. Records Created by the Office of the Secretary of the Navy, 1799-1874

1. Records Relating to Personnel

NAME INDEX TO PART (1799-1860) OF SERIES 26B. 1 vol. 2 in. — 1A

REGISTER OF JUDGMENTS AND SENTENCES OF COURTS-MARTIAL AND COURTS
OF INQUIRY. Aug. 1800-Jan. 1822. 1 vol. 2 in. — 1B
Arranged chronologically. Name index.

RECORDS OF PROCEEDINGS OF COURTS OF INQUIRY CONVENED UNDER THE
ACT OF JANUARY 16, 1857. Feb. 1857-Feb. 1859. 24 vols.
8 ft. — 1C
Arranged chronologically.

RECORD OF PROCEEDINGS OF A GENERAL COURT-MARTIAL IN THE CASE OF
COMMODORE CHARLES WILKES ("WILKES' TRIAL"). Mar. 9-Apr. 26, 1864.
3 vols. 8 in. — 1D
Arranged chronologically.

RECORD OF PROCEEDINGS OF A GENERAL COURT-MARTIAL IN THE CASE OF
FRANKLIN W. SMITH AND BENJAMIN G. SMITH ("CONTRACTORS' CASES,
SMITH TRIAL"). Sept. 15, 1864-Jan. 30, 1865. 10 vols. 3 ft. — 1E
Arranged chronologically. For a name index, see series 26A.

II. RECORDS CREATED BY THE OFFICE OF THE JUDGE ADVOCATE GENERAL,
1865-1866, 1877-1940

A. General Records, 1865-1866, 1879-1918

MEMORANDA, CIRCULARS, INSTRUCTIONS, AND REGULATIONS OF THE OFFICE
OF THE JUDGE ADVOCATE GENERAL ("SCRAP BOOKS"). 1893-1918.
2 vols. 7 in. — 19A
Arranged chronologically. Subject indexes. Included are some
announcements and directives of general information from other
Federal agencies.

B. Personnel Records, 1799-1943

1. Records Relating to General Courts-Martial, Courts of Inquiry,
Boards of Investigation, and Boards of Inquest, 1799-1943

NAME CARD INDEX TO SERIES 1E AND TO PARTS (1861-67) OF SERIES 26B AND 27. 1 ft.   26A

    This series was created by the Office of Naval Records and Library.

TRANSCRIPTS OF PROCEEDINGS OF GENERAL COURTS-MARTIAL AND COURTS OF INQUIRY. June 1799-Nov. 1867. ca. 180 vols. 58 ft.   26B

    Arranged by case number (1-4721). For name indexes, see series 1A and 26A. At the end of the series is a volume containing miscellaneous general courts-martial for the period 1839-68.

RECORDS OF PROCEEDINGS OF GENERAL COURTS-MARTIAL. Feb. 1866-Nov. 1942. 459 vols., ca. 2,100 looseleaf binders, folded and flat papers, and various other materials. 860 ft.   27

    For partial name index, see series 26A.

RECORDS OF PROCEEDINGS OF COURTS OF INQUIRY, BOARDS OF INVESTIGATION, AND BOARDS OF INQUEST. May 1866-Dec. 1942. 97 vols. and ca. 1,150 looseleaf binders. 405 ft.   30

TRANSCRIPT OF THE PROCEEDINGS OF AN INVESTIGATION CONDUCTED BY THE SOLICITOR RELATING TO THE CONSTRUCTION OF SUBMARINES BY THE CALIFORNIA SHIPBUILDING CO. 1916. 2 in.   41A

    Arranged chronologically.

RECORDS OF PROCEEDINGS IN INVESTIGATIONS BY COURTS OF INQUIRY AND BOARDS OF INVESTIGATION OF ACCIDENTS INVOLVING FOREIGN NATIONALS AND FOREIGN VESSELS. 1918-19. 5 in.   42A

LETTERS FROM THE SECRETARY OF THE NAVY INDICATING HIS ACTION WITH RESPECT TO RECORDS OF GENERAL COURTS-MARTIAL. Apr. 1924-Dec. 1942. 1 looseleaf binder and 7 folders. 1 ft.   45

TRANSCRIPT OF PROCEEDINGS OF A BOARD INVESTIGATING EXPLOSIONS AT THE NAVAL AMMUNITION DEPOT, LAKE DENMARK, N.J., ON JULY 15-16, 1926. 1926. 6 vols. and loose records. 2 ft.   45A

    Arranged chronologically. Table of contents in the first volume.

2. Records Relating to Summary Courts-Martial and Deck Courts, 1855-1930

SUMMARY SLIPS OF ABSTRACTS OF PROCEEDINGS OF DECK COURTS OF COAST GUARD PERSONNEL. 1917-19. 2 ft.   54A

    Arranged numerically by case number (1-996).

4. Other Personnel Records, 1860-1931

PERSONNEL REPORTS FROM COMMANDING OFFICERS. 1860-95. 26 ft.   64

C. Financial Records, 1869-1943

REGISTER OF CLAIMS FOR PERSONAL PROPERTY LOST ABOARD THE
U.S.S. CHARLESTON IN 1899 AND DURING THE SAN FRANCISCO FIRE
OF APRIL 1906. 1903-7. 1 vol. 1/2 in.   91A
   Arranged chronologically by date of receipt of claim. Name
index.

CARD ABSTRACTS OF CORRESPONDENCE RELATING TO CONTRACTS FOR THE
BUILDING AND REPAIR OF WORLD WAR I VESSELS. 1916-20. 3 in.   97A
   Arranged mainly by type of vessel, but partly arranged by
subject.

INFORMATION CARDS RELATING TO SETTLEMENTS WITH FORMER OWNERS OF
LAND IN NORFOLK, VA., PURCHASED BY THE NAVY DEPARTMENT.
1917-18. 1 ft.   98A
   Arranged in two subseries: (1) alphabetically by name of
former owner and (2) by letter-number designation of lot.

INDEX TO LEASE FILES. 1917-32. Cards 6 x 4 in. 3 ft.   102

REPORTS, MEMORANDA, TABLES, AND TRANSCRIPTS OF HEARINGS RELATING
TO PROPOSED LEGISLATION CONCERNING PAY, ALLOTMENTS, ALLOWANCES,
AND OTHER SERVICE BENEFITS. 1922-36. 3 in.   102A
   Arranged chronologically.

PLANS AND MEMORANDA RECEIVED FROM THE BUREAU OF CONSTRUCTION AND
REPAIR RELATING TO BIDS SUBMITTED FOR THE CONSTRUCTION OF DE-
STROYERS AND SUBMARINES. Aug. 1936. 9 in.   106A
   Arranged by type of vessel.

D. Records Relating to Patents, 1907-1942

TRANSCRIPT OF PROCEEDINGS OF A PATENT SUIT INVOLVING THE INTER-
NATIONAL TELEGRAPH CO. AND THE MARCONI WIRELESS TELEGRAPH CO.
OF AMERICA. 1917. 4 vols. 6 in.   108A
   Arranged chronologically. Table of contents in each volume.
This transcript is a printed copy.

E. Records Relating to Opinions and Decisions, 1846-1911

LETTERS FROM ATTORNEYS GENERAL ("OPINIONS OF ATTORNEYS GENERAL").
Sept. 1846-June 1903. 5 vols. 1 ft.   114

REGISTER OF OPINIONS OF THE ATTORNEY GENERAL. 1879-1906.
1 vol. 1/2 in. 114A
Entries arranged and numbered in chronological order. For
opinions, see series 114 and 119.

REGISTER OF SOLICITOR'S REPORTS AND OPINIONS. Dec. 1875-Apr. 1878.
1 vol. 2 in. 114B
Arranged chronologically. Name index.

F. Other Records, 1863-1929

SECRETARY OF THE NAVY CIRCULARS RELATING TO CONTRACTUAL REQUIRE-
MENTS FOR BUILDING VESSELS. 1901-16. 5 in. 125A

III. RECORDS OF BOARDS AND OTHER SPECIAL UNITS CONCERNED WITH
MATTERS UNDER THE COGNIZANCE OF THE JUDGE ADVOCATE GENERAL,
1885, 1896-1933

Board to Investigate a Contract With The American Wood Preserving Co.
Relating to Its Process of Preserving Wood

TRANSCRIPT OF PROCEEDINGS. Apr.-May 1885. 1 in. 129A
Arranged chronologically.

Board on Valuation of Commandeered Property

INFORMATION CARDS RELATING TO THE PURCHASE OF COMMANDEERED
PROPERTY. 1917-22. 2 ft. 135A
Arranged by name of place where land was located and thereunder
alphabetically by name of person from whom land was purchased.

www.ingramcontent.com/pod-product-compliance
Lightning Source LLC
Chambersburg PA
CBHW081723270326
41933CB00017B/3273